Kubernetes

A Step-By-Step Guide For Beginners To Build, Manage, Develop, and Intelligently Deploy Applications By Using Kubernetes

Author

Sheldon Miles

this book.

By reading this document, the reader agrees that under no circumstances is the author responsible for any losses, direct or indirect, that are incurred as a result of the use of information contained within this document, including, but not limited to, errors, omissions, or inaccuracies.

Table Of Contents

Introduction

Kubernetes has grown in popularity in recent years. The software developed by Google has become a favorite among developers. But what is it exactly? What is it capable of? How can one take advantage of its features?

Before we can actually dive into Kubernetes, we have to understand another concept first—containers.

Every year, the popularity of containers has been growing like wildfire. Attend any IT conference around the world and you would be hard-pressed to find one without having a segment on containers. More specifically, you are bound to find a segment or two on Docker.

So what exactly are containers?

Traditionally, when organizations ran applications, they would do so on physical servers. They could not define the boundaries of resources for applications using a physical server. Because of this, it was not easy to allocate resources to those applications.

For example, let us say that there are multiple applications running on a physical server. There would be instances where one application would take up too great a portion of the available resources while another would barely receive any. This means that one application would develop properly while another would continue to remain underdeveloped and eventually underperform. One solution to this problem was to add in more physical servers. But to many organizations, that does not solve the problem. Instead, it actually made the problem worse since adding more servers would mean increasing the budget of the organization. Maintaining a server can be expensive. Adding more servers creates a plethora of problems, especially if the organization or company chooses to scrap one of their projects later on. Any lost project means that all the expenses incurred up until that point are practically useless.

The alternative to a physical solution was a virtual one. Using a process of virtualization, multiple Virtual Machines (or VMs) could be run on the CPU of a single physical server. Each VM can be used for a particular application, isolating the VMs from each other and adding an extra layer of security. Any information used by one application cannot be accessed by another. Essentially, a Virtual Machine is a simulation of an actual machine, but it is created over a virtual space. You can then use the VM for various purposes such as application development.

Virtualization allows the applications to utilize resources more efficiently. It also provides scalability by allowing the applications to be updated and improved. It reduces hardware costs and you can work with multiple applications at the same time. The benefits of virtualization were many and this is what drew people towards VMs.

This is where containers come in. A container is a more lightweight version of a VM. Just like a VM, a container has its own filesystem, CPU, memory, and process space.

But earlier, we mentioned something about Docker. What is that, and how is it related to containers?

Docker is one of the core mechanisms that lies at the heart of container management. It has taken the present container technology to a whole new realm and, by doing so, it has made it easy to replicate and implement technology across different providers and environments. In short, Docker is a software that you can use to manage containers in Kubernetes. Since its inception, it has grown to become an important component in software development and updates.

All of this is possible because of the growth that the software industry has seen in recent times. Before the year 1999, the development of software used the waterfall development method. The method was crude and would not function in the fast-paced world that we live in today. With the technology that was used back then, it was the perfect way to create and develop new software. In the waterfall method, teams would get together and start making numerous arrangements in order to meet the requirements of the software. They would note down all the requirements, discuss with each other and, when satisfied that they had not overlooked anything, proceed to the development phase.

These development phases were independent from each other. The way to think of it is like looking at the different floors of a building. Each floor is part of the overall structure, yet they are not merged into each other. If you were the architect of the building and you had a great idea that you would like to implement on the 4th floor, then you wouldn't be able to do it unless you had completed the previous three floors. This is the same concept that applies to traditional software development. The developers had to start with the first stage and, when they were certain of the completion of that stage, they would progress to the next stage. Each stage had to be structurally sound and functionally viable if there was any chance to proceed further into the development of the software.

This is how developers had to complete the entire design of the software. Once that was done, they could move on to the next phase, coding and testing. The process was tedious, regimented, and rigid.

The biggest problem with the above method is that there was no room to adapt. For example, what if there was a flaw in the design? There was nothing that the developers were able to do at that time because the process did not allow them to discover that flaw. They had to wait until the software was used by the end user and even then, the user had to report the problem to the developers in order for them to actually spot it. This meant that the developers had to go back to the drawing board and redo the entire process again. By the time they had actually released the final version, the requirements of the users would change or a competitor would develop a better product based on the requirements.

To better understand the above process, let's go back to the example of the building that we had used. Imagine that you are building a hotel with six floors. You complete the building and then you realize that you have chosen the wrong theme or that certain parts of the building might not meet regulations or standards. If you were using the waterfall method, then you would have to destroy the entire building and then rebuild it again, taking the changes you had in mind into consideration. If you failed to meet another requirement the second time, then you would have to demolish the hotel again and start from the foundation.

Sounds rather tedious and expensive, doesn't it? And who is to say that while you are putting all the effort into building your hotel to a certain standard, someone else hasn't already built something to meet those very same standards? In that case, you have not only wasted time and effort (and not to mention a whole heap of patience), you have lost your target customers to your competition. What was the point of your efforts?

This was the same scenario that software developers faced. But things changed because of various innovations in technology.

One such innovation was the Internet of Things (or IoT), which made developing software more convenient. The idea behind the IoT was that numerous devices could be connected to each other and be able to communicate with each other without human intervention. This idea of interconnectivity would also play a vital in software development, as it would allow one feature of an application to work in sync with another feature.

Another innovation that provided benefits to software developers was the introduction of artificial intelligence (or AI). AI helps automate things and some forms of AI can even be programmed to make certain decisions. This gave software developers more freedom and convenience to develop and test out their products. Web applications were also introduced to cater to specific requirements. Each application would serve a purpose, so that software developers did not have to perform all the tasks. If there was a simple task that was best left to an automated process, then web applications would make sure that it was taken care of.

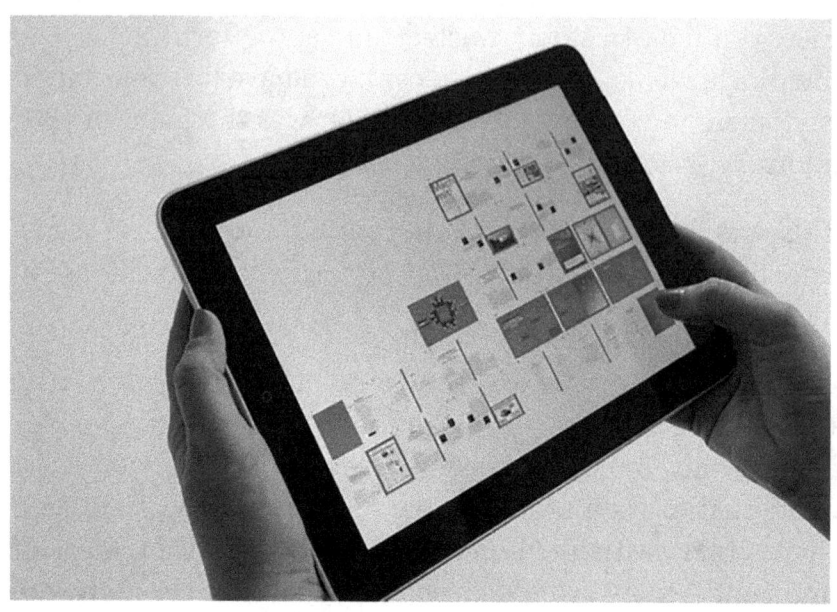

The Internet of Things (IoT) allowed better communication between various devices.

Let us take web development as an example. Today, you can simply use web applications to install a flash player or make custom modifications to your website. You don't have to do everything on your own. However, back before all of these incredible technological innovations were discovered, everything had to be done manually.

IoT, AI, and web applications are just some of the innovations that helped software developers greatly. These days, developers can test their design at any stage of the development process. They don't have to redo everything again.

Once again, let's go back to our wonderful hotel. This time, you don't have to wait for the hotel to complete construction in order to check its progress. When one floor is complete, you can check if it meets your requirements and standards. If you are satisfied, you can allow work on the next floor to begin.

Each stage in a piece of software could be properly analyzed before it could be deployed. At the same time, you have software like Docker that adds another layer of convenience to software developers by taking existing technology and allowing it to be replicated across various providers and environments.

In the three decades leading up to 2019, a lot has changed in the way that software developers can carry out their work. Before the concept of Kubernetes arrived to make things easier, developers had to use a long method to create their software.

The introduction of Kubernetes, especially the concept of containers, made things even more convenient. In a production environment, you often need to ensure that there is no downtime. When one container goes down, you would like another container to take over. However, it would be more convenient if there was a system that could handle all the work instead. This allows you to have the freedom to focus on other problems that you have to deal with during the software development process. This is where Kubernetes comes to the rescue.

Kubernetes is an open-source platform that is used for managing computerized services and workloads. It facilitates automation for convenience and offers more ways to configure the work. Because Kubernetes is an open-source program, it has numerous tools, support, and services. It also has a large community that constantly helps developers in numerous stages of their software development. The project was open-sourced by Google in 2014. The multi-billion-dollar software giant used its decades of experience for the final product.

But understanding Kubernetes is just the first step. In order to completely work with the system, we need to know more about its constituent parts. For that reason, we shall start off by understanding containers and then move on to the various components of Kubernetes.

Once that is accomplished, we can then move on to delving deep into the world of Kubernetes, looking at how you can work with containers, DevOps, and many other features. We will also look at storage, understand resources, and so much more.

So without further delay, let's get started.

Chapter 1: Getting Started With

Kubernetes

Before we break down Kubernetes, let's look at containers and try to understand the many features that this concept provides developers.

An Overview of Containers

At the core of containers are features called control groups (or cgroups). Cgroups are important because they allow the host to limit and also share resources that each container utilizes. This is important for several reasons, including proper allocation of resources to ensure that each container functions smoothly

It also impacts security and prevents certain attacks, such as denial-of-service attacks. A distributed denial-of-service attack, or DDoS, is a cyberattack in which the attacker removes access to a certain machine or software. This way, the real owner of those components might find out that the work he or she has been performing becomes unavailable to him or her. This allows the attacker to carry out changes, install malicious software, and cause other forms of harm. In some cases, they can indefinitely disrupt the services of the host.

But those are not the only benefits that containers are able to provide. Containers allow for easy application creation and their deployment. Containers can increase efficiency and make work faster for the developer.

Containers are also able to provide constant development, integration, and deployment features. This allows developers to receive reliable and frequent build and deployment. They are also able to perform their tasks with quick and easy rollbacks.

When developers are using containers, they have a certain consistency across platforms. They can run, test, and produce their applications the same way on the laptop or other computing device as they do in the cloud. This is because they have access to the containers no matter where they access them from.

Resources are isolated and this allows for users to predict the performance of the application. When they are able to predict performance, they can make corrections whenever necessary and are able to get an overall idea of what the end result might turn out to be.

There is more efficiency in the way the resources are utilized as well. Typically, working outside of containers might lead to wasting resources, but containers ensure that applications work with a specific number of resources.

While recognizing some of the features of containers, it is also important to grasp the concept of namespace. Namespace is an important feature in Kubernetes that allots resources to various containers. It also connects various processes together. This allows different processes to interact with each other efficiently. Namespaces also place a limit on the level of visibility that one process has on other ID components, filesystems, and networking. A container process then becomes restricted. This allows for each container to work independently without any outside influence or effects, which could affect the integrity and quality of the process.

Furthermore, users can also utilize union file systems. To understand what a union is, we have to look at the game Tetris. This might take you by surprise, but there is a reason for using this example. What union does is take the files and directories of different file systems and creates one single file system comprising of the individual file systems. Think of each file system as one part of a Tetris block. Each block is of a different shape, but if you get them together, they form straight rows. However, if you break apart the rows, you can still get the individual parts. This is the same with union. You can still utilize each of the individual components, but they are all stacked together to form a single file system.

This is convenient because having different file systems means that work becomes more complicated and it is longer to perform a task.

So the big question is, why should you use Docker?

Containers on their own are not a new technology and have actually been around for many years. There are many applications that can run it. However, what truly sets Docker apart from other applications is the ease of use it has brought to the community. Docker promotes the use of Continuous Deployment and Continuous Integration. This means that even when you have to troubleshoot something or there are certain updates you have to run, there is no delay in progress. These methods, when utilized properly, can have a great impact on your software product's results and quality.

Concepts of Kubernetes

While getting familiar with Kubernetes, you might need to know certain concepts, lest you become confused by the jargon that gets thrown around when referring to Kubernetes. Here are some important concepts that you need to be aware of.

kubelet

A kubelet is an agent that ensures that each node on the cluster is running successfully. This further ensures that containers are successfully running within a pod. The way Kubernetes does this is by taking PodSpecs that are available through various mechanisms and that each container that was part of the PodSpecs is running smoothly and successfully. A kubelet does not manage any container that was not specifically created in Kubernetes.

kube-proxy

This is a proxy network that works with each node in the cluster you manage. A kube-proxy also helps nodes maintain their network rules. These rules are important if you would like to allow network communication from outside sessions.

Node

The smallest unit used in computing in Kubernetes is called a node. Essentially, it represents one machine in your cluster. In a production process, a node either represents a physical machine that is located somewhere or a virtual machine that you are making use of. When you think of a machine as a node, then you don't have to worry about its characteristics.

Now, you simply have to think of a machine as a collection of CPU and GPU. That way, you can substitute one node with any other node in Kubernetes.

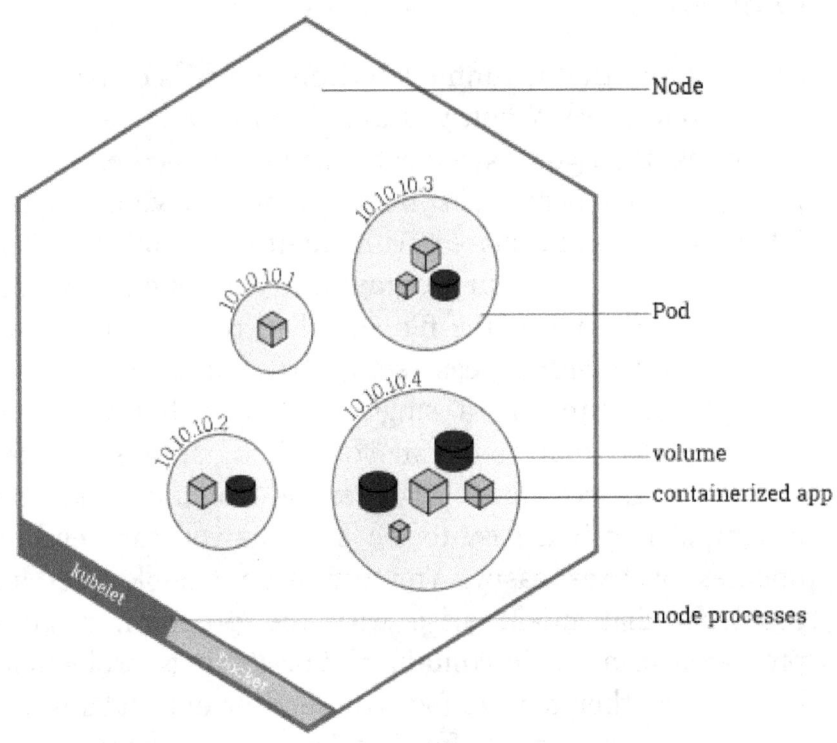

This is what a typical node looks like.

Cluster

Although people find working with individual nodes to be rather useful, it is not how work is carried out in Kubernetes. You usually work with a cluster, rather than worry about an individual node. In Kubernetes, nodes come together and pool their computing resources to form a powerful cluster or resources. When you deploy work in a cluster, the cluster itself automatically and intelligently distributes the work among the various nodes in the cluster. In the end, it does not matter which node is working on which task. The focus is on the end result and the fastest way to reach it.

Containers

Any program that is running on Kubernetes is converted to Linux containers. When you are able to containerize your programs, then you have created self-contained executable packages. This means that you can bundle up your program into a single file and share it with others on the internet. This allows people to use your program with convenience. Anyone can simply download the file and then run it in their own infrastructure with an easy setup procedure. You can add multiple programs to a single container, but it is best recommended that you limit yourself by adding just one program per container. If a single container has one program, then it is easy to focus on, as you can send out updates or fixes easily. You can even troubleshoot any problems that might arise with the program. Multiple programs in a single container makes things problematic because you then have to focus on sending out updates for a single program without affecting the other programs.

Pod

One of the other features of Kubernetes is that it does not run containers directly. It uses a mechanism called pods where multiple containers are stored. All the containers in the pod will share the same network and resources. Because the containers share a pod, they can easily communicate with each other, should such a need arise. However, here is where things get better. Even though they can communicate with each other, there can be a level of isolation, as well. This means that one container cannot heavily affect another, which might cause program issues.

Deployment

Even though pods are considered to be the basic unit of computation, they are not usually launched into a cluster directly. This is because you could have multiple replicas of the pods. This is done because when one pod is bearing a heavy load, you can easily shift to the replica and focus your work there. When you have multiple replicas, then the main job of a deployment is to determine which pod or its replicas should be allowed to run at a particular time. This is done in order to ensure that pods that cannot work efficiently do not take resources that other pods could be using. Deployment also helps you with automation.

Components of Kubernetes

Now that you have understood some of the basic concepts of Kubernetes, let's look at some of its important components.

etcd

This component stores all the configuration information that each of the nodes in the cluster can use. The key value store of this node is highly available, making it accessible by multiple nodes. Because the information contained within the node is sensitive, it can only be accessed by a Kubernetes API.

API Server

It is important to know that Kubernetes is an API server. What exactly is an API? The name is an abbreviation of *application program interface* and it is a compilation of tools, protocols, and routines that are essential for software development. We are going to discuss more about API further into the book. But essentially, developers can also use APIs when they have to program components required for developing a graphical user interface (GUI). A good API allows developers to create their software or program by providing all the necessary foundational tools. A developer simply has to put the blocks together.

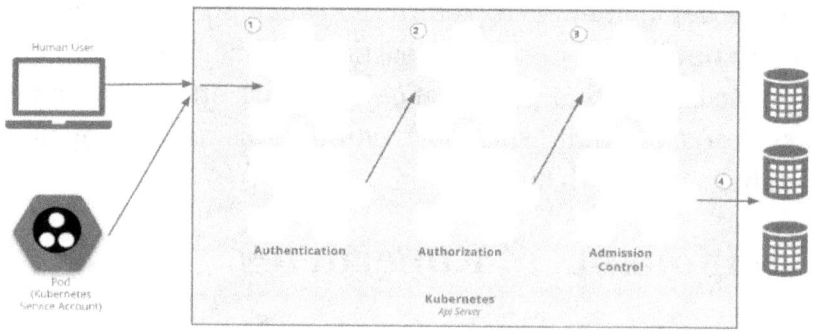

This is what a typical API structure looks like in Kubernetes.

Controller Manager

This component is responsible for controlling those functions of the API that makes sure that the state of a particular cluster is normal. The controller manager also helps perform various tasks.

Scheduler

This is an essential component of Kubernetes. This component helps distribute the workload efficiently. It is also responsible for tracking the utilization of the workload. If another node might require a workload, then it ensures that the node receives it. In this way, the system functions without many issues.

Kubernetes Resources

Kubernetes also provides you with various resources and features to help you to work with the various components we had discussed above. Some of these features are:

Load balancing and Service Discovery

When you would like to look at a particular container, you can encourage Kubernetes to reveal it to you using an IP address or DNS name. In the off chance that the traffic to that particular container is high, Kubernetes is capable of distributing the network traffic so that the process of deployment is stable.

Freedom of Storage

Kubernetes also allows you to utilize and mount a storage system that you prefer. This allows you to make use of public cloud providers, local storage systems, and more.

Rollbacks and Rollouts Automation

Kubernetes enables you to automate rollbacks and rollouts. Let us take an example of how this works. Let's say that you have three pods with a copy of the first version of your application: Version 1.0. The versions in all three pods are the same. The reason there are three pods is so that if one pod needs to undergo maintenance, then the traffic can be routed to the other copies of your version.

You have added improvements to your version and you are ready to push out Version 2.0. Kubernetes creates a new pod with the image (app) of your new version, Version 2.0. When Kubernetes confirms that the image is good to go, it removes the previous pod that you had created. This way, you now have a Version 2.0 and two pods of Version 1.0. When the second copy of Version 2.0 is created and is ready to accept traffic, another pod of Version 1.0 is pushed out. You now have two pods of Version 2.0 and only one pod of Version 1.0. The above process is repeated until there are no more pods featuring Version 1.0. You have successfully launched Version 2.0.

Self-Healing

This is another important feature of Kubernetes that is typically not found on other platforms. Kubernetes can kill containers that do not respond well to your predetermined health-checks, replace containers that are not successful, and even restart containers that do not function properly.

Information Management

Kubernetes also allows you to manage and store sensitive information without worrying about the security of that information.

Advantages of Kubernetes

Kubernetes seems pretty complex doesn't it? After learning about its concepts and components, you might be left wondering—why exactly do people like working with Kubernetes anyways? What makes it special?

Reduced Expenses

To begin with, one of the biggest advantages that any company is looking for is reducing expenses. Containers are isolated "packages" and these packages include all the required components that the application needs to properly execute and run. Multiple containers can share the same network connection and OS. This setup makes it more efficient to utilize resources compared to a scenario where there is a virtual machine with its own OS for each application. Containers are designed to be lightweight and consume fewer resources, enabling you to save on data center costs and hardware.

Without Kubernetes, you might incur a lot of expenditure trying to set up real and virtual machines to handle all the work you want to do.

Portability and Ease of Use

The isolated arrangement of containers allows you to run your software across environments in a consistent manner. This means that Kubernetes is isolated to an online platform. You don't have to carry with you in a device. Whether you are using your own laptop or you are making use of a public cloud service, you can run across all the platforms without losing your data or having it affected in a negative way.

Containers can also be copied to test, develop, integrate and set the programs to live environments reliably and quickly. This greatly speeds and simplifies the program development and release processes, resulting in speedier market availability. This in turn offers developers more opportunities. For example, consider their overall business goals. They are probably thinking of improving customer relations, which is extremely important if they would like to garner more customers for their product. When you are using Kubernetes, you can respond to customer complaints and suggestions quickly, which will make your customers really happy about your responses.

It Has an Impressive Heritage

Think about it: with Kubernetes, you are using a tool that has been developed by Google engineers with years of experience on their resumes. At the same time, Kubernetes wasn't built overnight. Google developers have been honing its application development capabilities for more than a decade. Once they realized the potential that Kubernetes could offer, they released it to the world. The result is their individual and the entire organization's experience put together in a platform that is designed to help developers in the best way possible.

Modularity and Scalability

Since your typical container is lightweight, developers can create one within seconds. This enables them to scale instantly, which is especially helpful. An example is if they would like to react seamlessly to unexpected website traffic load. Containers also make it really easy to take your application and break it down into individual parts, each of the parts having their own functions. You can even have your databases in one container while your application is in another container. Docker also lets you create a connection between these containers so that it is easy to scale or update the containers individually. This advantage becomes even better when you use them with other services, offering you even more benefits.

Starting Up a New Kubernetes Cluster

We have understood various concepts of Kubernetes. We have even looked at some of its components. Now it is time to get started on the platform.

To start working with Kubernetes, we are first going to use Google's Cloud services. When we do this, Google provides us a platform to work with, and we install Kubernetes into that platform. All you have to do is simply head over to this link: https://cloud.google.com/kubernetes-engine/

The link you use takes you to Google Compute Engine, or GCE. If you are wondering what GCE is, it is the service component of Google Cloud and the platform that allows you to use Kubernetes.

Think of the above situation like using an image editor. You can't directly edit the image. You need a platform to upload the image and make changes to it. Similarly, Google is the platform that will allow you to install and work with Kubernetes.

When you first start Kubernetes, you will notice that there are a lot of features to work with. But we are going to ignore all of that and focus on simply booting up your Kubernetes environment.

To begin with, we need to make sure that the environment that we are using is ready. To do so, we need to update Kubernetes packages (it is better to do this manually). By updating the packages, you are installing any new features that aren't already present.

Use the below command first.

$ sudo apt-get update

Your next step is to install curl and Python if they are not available:

$ sudo apt-get install python

$ sudo apt-get install curl

You might also have to install the gcloud SDK:

$ curl https://sdk.cloud.google.com | bash

Source: (Baier, 2017)

For the next procedure, you will have to configure the GCP account information. Your GCP is the Google Cloud Platform that you are using to work with Kubernetes smoothly. By using the below command, you can directly open a browser window that you can use in your Google Cloud account and then authorize the SDK.

$ gcloud auth login

--no-launch-browser

PRO TIP: Some users might experience a problem with the login process or they might prefer to use another browser. In such cases, you can simply use the below command:

--no-launch-browser

Once done, you can copy and paste the URL in the browser of your choice. For the next step, you can log in easily to your Google Cloud account. Head over to the **permissions** page and then click **Allow**. Once done, you will receive an authorization code that you simply have to enter into the area (called shell) where it is required. Usually, the shell will display a prompt for the password.

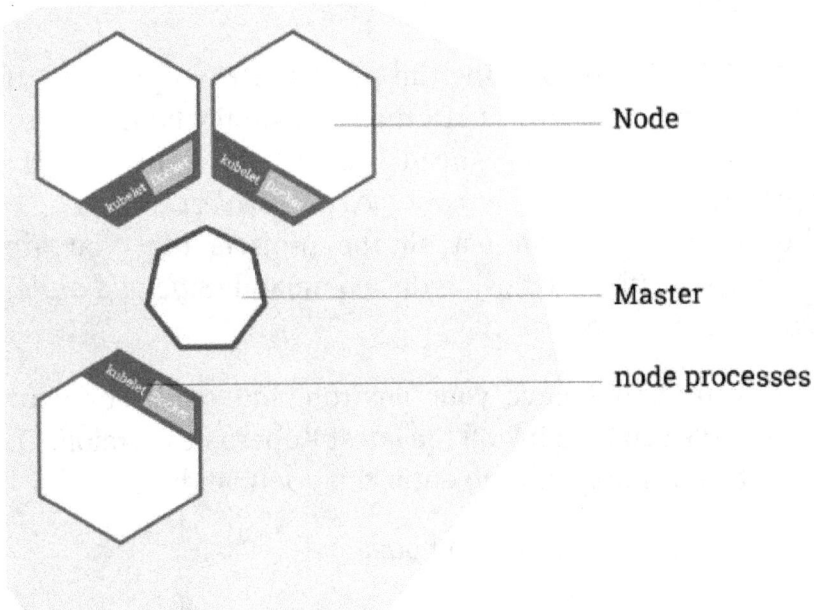

Kuberneters cluster

This is a typical Kubernetes cluster.

You should be presented with a default project. However, you can still verify if it is in the default state by entering the below command:

$ gcloud config list project

If you prefer, you can also set and modify a new default project.

$ gcloud config set project <PROJECT ID>

Remember that the above code includes the project ID and not the project name. Most users end up entering the name of the project accidentally and that does nothing to the command.

PRO TIP: Trouble finding the project ID? No problem. If you ever lost your project ID, then you simply boot up your browser and then head over to this URL: *https://console.developers.google.com/project.*
Alternatively, you can list all the projects that you are working on actively by using this command: *$ gcloud alpha projects list*

Now, you should have your environment ready for your project. We can then install the latest Kubernetes version. To do that, you simply have to enter this command:

$ curl -sS https://get.k8s.io | bash

Source: (Baier, 2017)

It might take a couple of minutes to download Kubernetes, depending on your connection speed. In earlier versions, Kubernetes would automatically load the *kube-up.sh* script and then start building your cluster. However, in the new version, you have to enter the script yourself. By default, you should be using Google Cloud, in which case, you should enter the below command:

$ kubernetes/cluster/kube-up.sh

Source: (Baier, 2017)

Once you run the above script, Google Cloud will begin to run a prerequisite check. This should not take a long time, and the step is important to make sure that all the necessary components are installed properly. If the check is successful, then you will be notified that all the components are updated and that SDK is installed. If not, you will receive a prompt that will either tell you to perform an update or install a particular component.

Once that above process has been completed, Google Cloud will then check to see if any pieces of a cluster are already running. Wait for Google to complete the step and then you are ready to create your own cluster.

In the last step, Google Cloud will also create nodes and minions for our cluster. It is within these parameters that our containers will be able to run.

When everything is created, the cluster is ready. If everything goes well, then you should receive an IP address for the master. Do note that configurations along with your cluster management credentials are saved in the following format:

home/<Username>/.kube/config:

Once the cluster is ready, then the *kubectl.sh* script will be used to validate the cluster. This script counts the number of nodes that are discovered and are registered. It also lets you know if any of the nodes are in a ready state.

The script will then run *kubectl cluster-info*.

Let us now look at your Kubernetes UI:

Open the browser of your preference and then enter the below code:

https://<your master ip>/ui/

The certificate of the website is usually signed by itself. You might have to ignore the warnings that your browser presents to you before you are able to proceed. A login box will then pop up. In this box, you will be able to use the credentials that you had received when Kubernetes was installing. If you feel like you don't remember your credentials, then do not worry, simply use the blow command:

$ kubectl config view

When you have logged into your account, you will then be presented with a dashboard. You might notice that your dashboard is empty. But this is normal since you do not have any workloads running. You might see a big box at the top that has the message "There is nothing to display here." Some users might mistake this as an error message, so do not be alarmed or worried.

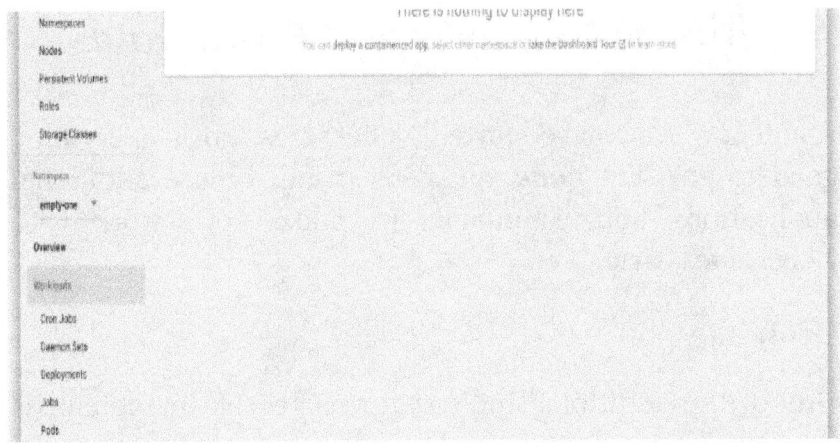

Don't worry if you see this message in the beginning.

You can click on the **Nodes** section on the left menu column (see image above). You will be presented with a set of metrics on the current nodes.

At the top of the page, you will notice two boxes. The left box will be titled "CPU usage history" and will present the aggregate CPU usage details. It allows you to manage the programs running on your laptop or computer so that you do not overload your machine. To the right of the "CPU usage history" section, you will find the "Memory usage history" section. This section will let you know how much memory is utilized at a given point in time, which will allow you to manage your workloads. When you are able to understand when you utilized a lot of memory, you will be able to better manage your Workload.

Additional Features and Commands

Right now, you have started Kubernetes. So is everything good to go? Not quite yet. Let's install or use additional applications and commands to make your work with Kubernetes easier.

Grafana

One of the additional tools that you receive by default is Grafana. This is a metric tool that allows you to use a special dashboard to view your metrics in a cluster node. You can easily install it on the app page. Just follow the below link:

https://grafana.com/grafana/plugins/grafana-kubernetes-app

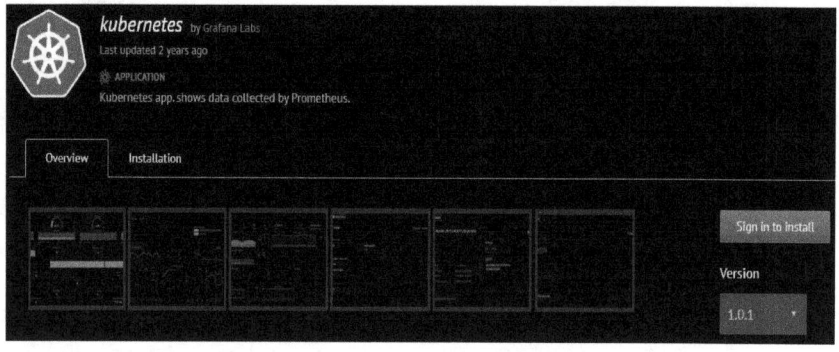

This is what the Grafana download screen looks like.

Command Line

You can use the kubectl script to explore the commands that are used for the workloads and clusters. If you would like to access it, then you simply have to use the below folder:

/kubernetes/client/bin

We are going to be visiting the above section numerous times in this book, so make sure you familiarize yourself with it. Let's set up the environment for it, as well. Simply use the below command lines to get started:

$ export PATH=$PATH:/<Path where you downloaded K8s>/kubernetes/client/bin

$ chmod +x /<Path where you downloaded K8s>/kubernetes/client/bin

Source: (Baier, 2017)

In the above command, the term "K8" simply refers to Kubernetes. Often, people prefer to use the short version instead of the entire term. But do not use the short version in your command lines! For example, don't simply type *"Path where you downloaded K8s."* Enter the actual path name.

PRO TIP: Usually, Kubernetes is found within the home folder. If you like, you can also download your Kubernetes folder outside the home folder. You can do so by simply changing the above command line as you would like.

Once you have set up kubectl, you are free to perform necessary tasks using it. Currently, we do not have any applications running on it yet, so we won't be able to explore it too much. However, we can look at two important commands.

If you would like to look at info about your cluster, then you can use the below command:

$ kubectl cluster-info

You can also see all the services, replication controllers, pods, and other functions that are currently running.

To list all the nodes in the cluster: *$ kubectl get nodes*

Checking the events in the cluster: *$ kubectl get events*

View the services that are running in your cluster: *$ kubectl get services*

First Cluster

There you have it! Your very first Kubernetes cluster. But our work is not done yet. There are a few more commands that you have to run. Let's go through them one by one.

Running Services

Time to delve deeper into the new cluster that we have set up and some of its important services. By default, machines or nodes are named using the prefix *kubernetes-*. You can change the prefix if you like by simply using the command:

$KUBE_GCE_INSTANCE_PREFIX

Make sure that you enter the command before starting the cluster. Take note of the cluster that we have just started. It should ideally be named *kubernetes-master*. This makes it easy to follow the commands presented in this book and it prevents any confusion as you work with Kubernetes. After you have mastered the platform, you can tweak various commands the way you see fit. Now we need to start SSH, which is a Secure Shell. This protocol gives remote administration privileges to users so that they can control and modify servers using the internet.

Syntax: *$ gcloud compute ssh --zone "<your gce zone>" "kubernetes-master"*

We need to log in at this point and once we have done so, we receive a shell prompt. Using the *docker* command:

$ sudo docker ps --format 'table {{.Image}}t{{.Status}}'

You might notice that there are several containers that are already running, even though we haven't deployed any applications. This might seem a bit confusing to people, but let us examine each container so that you are aware of what is happening in front of you,

fluentd-gcp

Any cluster log files are collected by this container. Once they are collected, the container sends it to Google's Cloud Logging service.

node-problem-detector

It is important to have a container that is capable of detecting issues at the kernel layer and within the hardware. This is why you have this container.

rescheduler

This container plays a vital role in ensuring that all the critical parts are running. In the event that some of the vital parts or components do not receive enough resources, then it makes sure that pods that are less important or critical receive fewer resources until another plan has been set up.

glbc

This is an add-on container. Its main purpose is to provide assistance to Google Cloud Layer 7 in order to balance loads using a special feature known as *Ingress*. Layer 7 is the load balancer provided by Google. A load balancer ensures that traffic is distributed between various servers. If a particular server is taking too much traffic at the cost of another server, then the load balancer will ensure that it minimizes that traffic in order to give other servers the required load. But hold on. How is it that you are using multiple servers? Well, in order to create containers to hold your applications, you will be creating Virtual Machines (VM). The VMs are basically virtual servers. The more VMs you have, the more virtual servers you are going to be managing.

kube-addon-manager

If you would like to add any changes to the */etc/kubernetes/addons* directory, then you have to make use of this container. In other words, all the containers that you see in this list have certain restrictions. You cannot simply access them and make changes. To do so, you will be using the kube-addon-manager container. An add-on is an extra container that is provided by Google. For example, *glbc* is an add-on (as we saw earlier). Some people wonder why Google provides add-ons. The best way to understand that is to think of your internet browser. If you are using one of the latest iterations of your browser, then it includes a Flash player by default. This player is an add-on and is used to watch videos and interact with objects on the internet. You can always turn it off if you prefer, but it definitely plays an important role in your internet browsing experience. The same scenario applies to add-ons provided in Kubernetes.

etcd-empty-dir-cleanup

To clean up any empty keys in etcd, then use this container.

kube-controller-manager

This container is used to discover, monitor, and manage new nodes. Additionally, you can also use the container to perform various cluster functions. It also updates endpoints and allows you to manage them.

kube-apiserver

Whenever you wish to run the API server, then this container helps you do that.

kube-scheduler

When you are working with Kubernetes, you might often run into unscheduled pods. This container ensures that you can bind the pods to certain nodes. The best way to understand this is to think of containers and pods. We know that containers are organized into pods. Each pod is placed on groups of resources called "nodes." The kube-scheduler ensures that each pod finds a suitable set of resources on a node. It does this to ensure that a pod does not consume more resources than is necessary or have too little resources to function properly.

etcd

Kubernetes presents you with the etcd software. You can run the software using this container. The software itself is important for storing, updating, and retrieving various parts of Kubernetes, or K8s.

pause

You can set up and mention the networking resource limit for each pod using this container.

PRO TIP: If you intended to exit SSH, then you simply have to enter *exit* at the prompt.

Because we have not started any applications using any of the clusters, we are not able to see any pods. However, there are already certain pods that are running within Kubernetes. We can access and view these pods by simply mentioning the *kube-system* namespace.

Use this command in order to look at the various K8 resources: *--namespace=kubesystem*

Once you enter the command, you might notice something like the below:

etcd-empty-dir-cleanup-kubernetes-master

etcd-server-events-kubernetes-master

etcd-server-kubernetes-master

fluentd-cloud-logging-kubernetes-master

fluentd-cloud-logging-kubernetes-minion-group-xxxx

heapster-v1.2.0-xxxx

kube-addon-manager-kubernetes-master

kube-apiserver-kubernetes-master

kube-controller-manager-kubernetes-master

kube-dns-xxxx

kube-dns-autoscaler-xxxx

kube-proxy-kubernetes-minion-group-xxxx

kube-scheduler-kubernetes-master

kubernetes-dashboard-xxxx

l7-default-backend-xxxx

l7-lb-controller-v0.8.0-kubernetes-master

monitoring-influxdb-grafana-xxxx

node-problem-detector-v0.1-xxxx

rescheduler-v0.2.1-kubernetes-master

Source: (Baier, 2017)

You might recognize the first six lines, as they refer to those services that are already running on the master. You might also notice a few additional services. Let us look at each one of them.

kube-dns-xxxx: Provides you with service discovery features and DNS.

kubernetes-dashboard-xxxx: This is the main interface that you will be using in Kubernetes.

l7-default-backend-xxxx: This command specifies the load balancing backend.

heapster-v1.2.0-xxxx: Gives you access to the database found within *Heapster*

Source: (Baier, 2017)

If we run SSH into a minion, then you might come across services that you hadn't seen before. Let us look at them:

kubedns

The main purpose of this container is to keep monitoring the endpoint resources and services in Kubernetes. If there are any changes in the DNS, then those changes are synced throughout the database.

kube-dnsmasq

DNS caching is important to speed up certain processes. This container helps you with the caching process.

dnsmasq-metrics

In order to provide reporting features, you can use this container.

l7-defaultbackend

A backend service allows you to examine a particular process and make vital changes to it. However, in order to access the backend, you need a special container for it, which is in the form of l7-defaultbackend.

exechealthz

Checking the health of your pod keeps you updated about progress. You can use this container to form health checks whenever you like.

heapster_grafana

Made for monitoring resources and using them efficiently.

addon-resizer

Important if you would like to scale your containers.

heapster

Analytics and monitoring is possible with this container.

kube-proxy

This container ensures that you have a service proxy and network for your cluster. It is the responsibility of this container to make sure that service traffic is being utilized by those workloads that are running in your cluster.

cluster-proportional-autoscaler

This container works almost like the addon-resizer container. The only difference is that you can use this container in order to scale your other containers in proportion to the size of your cluster.

Cluster Tear

Feels good setting up your first cluster, doesn't it? That's only the beginning. When we were talking about Kubernetes, we mentioned using it on GCE. However, GCE is not the only platform you have available for you. Before you start working on GCE, you might want to look at some of these other platforms.

So what are the other providers that we can work with? Let us examine some of them.

Provider	Value of KUBERNETES _PROVIDER	Type
Google Compute Engine	gce	Public Cloud
Google Container Engine	gke	Public Cloud
Amazon Web Services	aws	Public Cloud
Microsoft Azure	azure	Public Cloud
VMware vSphere	vsphere	Private cloud/on-premise virtualization

Hashicorp Vagrant	vagrant	Virtual development environment
Libvirt running CoreOS	libvirt-coreos	Virtualization management tool
Canonical Juju	juju	OS service orchestration tool

Try to look at different platforms and see which one works for you.

AWS - Getting Started

Some users who are reading this book might not be using GCE. They might be making use of the AWS platform. While most of the Kubernetes commands are the same for GCE and AWS, there are a few changes in the cluster setup process. Let's try and look at the setup process in AWS. If you are making use of GCE, you can choose to skip this section entirely.

Setting Up a Cluster on AWS

Let us look at how you can set up a cluster on AWS. In order to make your work more smooth, you need to have the AWS Command Line Interface (CLI) installed. In order to do this, you can simply visit the below website:

http://docs.aws.amazon.com/cli/latest/userguide/installing.html#install-bundle-other-os

It is also important for you to have the configuration documentation, this you can find in the below link:

http://docs.aws.amazon.com/cli/latest/userguide/cli-chap-getting-started.html

Once you have completed the installation, then you have to begin bnyu entering the command line:

$ export KUBERNETES_PROVIDER=aws

Then you can spin up the cluster using the below command:

$ kube-up.sh

As with the set up that we accomplished using GCE, you might require a few minutes before the system is ready for you to use.

We will not have to SSH. To do this, you simply have to enter:

$ ssh -v -i /home/<username>/.ssh/kube_aws_rsa ubuntu@<Your master IP>

Once the setup has been completed, you will be asked to enter your login credentials. If you are not aware of them or have forgotten them, then you can quickly retrieve them at:

$ kubectl config view

When you first enter the platform, you will have to create your index. You do not have to worry about the default layout and metrics that show up. Head over to the Time-field name and then enter *@timestamp* as your preferred option. Next, simply click on the **Create** button and then you will be directed to the settings section of your index page. Head over to the **Discover** tab (which will be located on the top of the page) and then you will be able to examine your dashboard in detail.

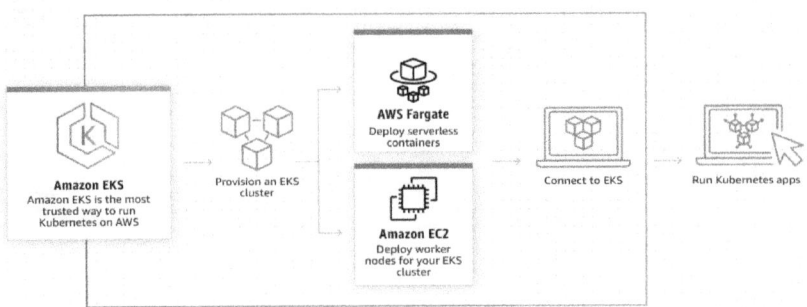

Amazon's Kubernetes platform has its own set of features.

Cluster Tear Down

I have just provided a brief introduction to AWS. However, I am going to be using the GCE cluster to explain the points and work presented in the rest of the book. This is because GCE is more widely used and I think provides the best features and experience.

Beginning From the Basics

Type	Protocol	Port Range	Source
All Traffic	All	All	{This SG ID (Master SG)}
All Traffic	All	All	{Node SG ID}
SSH	TCP	22	{Your Local Machine's IP}
HTTPS	TCP	443	{Range allowed to access K8s API and UI}

But what if you wanted to start from scratch? Would you be able to do it? Thankfully, you can. Make sure that you are using the latest Kubernetes version. If you are, then all you have to do is make sure that you have at least 1 GB of RAM, since you might require enough processing power to run the platform smoothly. You should also ensure that all the nodes are connected to each other via the network.

To begin with, you need to make sure that you have the following ports:

Installing Components

At this point, we need to install various Kubernetes components.

Step 1

You need to update the package. You will also need to install the apt-transport-https package. This allows you to download various files and components from sources that have HTTPS in their URL.

To perform the update, you simply have to use:

$ apt-get update

$ apt-get install -y apt-transport-https

Step 2

You will then have to make sure that you have the public key from Google Cloud. You can easily get the public key by the command:

$ curl -s https://packages.cloud.google.com/apt/doc/apt-key.gpg | apt-key add -

Step 3

It is time to create a source list. This list allows you to download various packages from a certain editor. You can even choose your favorite editor, should you have one.

$ vi /etc/apt/sources.list.d/kubernetes.list

Step 4

When you have the file, then you simply have to use the below command and then save.

deb http://apt.kubernetes.io/ kubernetes-xenial main

Step 5

Just to make sure everything has been performed properly, update your sources.

$ apt-get update

Then you have to install key components of Kubernetes and Docker. To do so:

$ apt-get install -y docker.io

$ apt-get install -y kubelet kubeadm kubectl kubernetes-cni

Next Steps

Whether you choose to use GCE or set up Kubernetes elsewhere from scratch, the next steps you have to take are the same. Let's look at them.

Master Set Up

We need to then initialize the master. To do so, simply enter:

$ kubeadm init

Node Joining

Time to join the nodes! You only need a simple join command that the nodes can use.

$ kubeadm join --token=<some token> <master ip address>

Source: (Baier, 2017)

Network

In order for the pods to communicate with each other, you might need a layer of networking capabilities. For this, you might need to get the right plugin. To check available plugins, you can visit this link:

http://kubernetes.io/docs/admin/addons/

For the sake of this book, we are going to use calico. You can create components from calico by visiting the URL below:

http://docs.projectcalico.org/v1.6/getting-started/kubernetes/installation/hosted/kubeadm/calico.yaml

Get the required files from the above link and then run the below command:

$ kubectl apply -f calico.yaml

You might require a few minutes in order to properly complete the setup process. You can check the process by:

$ kubectl get pods --namespace=kube-system

Cluster Joining

In order to join any cluster that we have created or is existing, then you have to simply use:

$ kubeadm join --token=<some token> <master ip address>

And with that, you have completed the installation process of Kubenetes. Time to move into DevOps.

Chapter 2: Getting Into DevOps

DevOps is an important concept to understand when dealing with Kubernetes. It isn't a software or program. Rather, it is a kind of work structure that allows you to create and launch your applications effectively. It is important to know about DevOps because without it, you are going to spend endless hours working on Kubernetes without having a proper working structure.

But before we can learn about DevOps, we need to understand the concept of microservices.

What Is Microservice?

Kubernetes provides a facility service that is highly native and is possible through the DNS service that comes with the platform. You will not require any extra setup process to install all the microservices within the cluster. This allows the user to put his or her focus entirely on the dependencies and definitions of the service without having to worry about the smaller configurations required for microservice setup.

So what exactly is a microservice?

A microservice is a component that contains everything from the framework, platform, operating system, dependencies, and runtime, all packaged as a single unit of executable file. Some might often confuse a microservice with a container. But the difference is that containers feature certain logic that is required to perform a task by using minimal resources.

One of the key features of microservices is that they are independent and autonomous. This makes them easy to monitor. You can easily identify faulty services and then replace them without affecting other components. You can also scale-out a particular microservice that is in demand. This allows you to avoid launching multiple versions of the application server. If there is a load shift and other components of the application are put into focus, a previous microserver will be scaled-in.

If you had to distill the meaning of microservice into a simple form, then you can say that it is a piece of software that can be executed on its own. You do not need a complicated interface in order to access it. Typically, you can work with a microservice using HTTP.

You might think that a microservice is something that only small entities use in order to make things more convenient for them. But that is not true. Big names such as Amazon, eBay, Netflix, PayPal, Twitter, and The Guardian have all made use of microservices in order to make things more efficient for them.

But how does this work? Let's take an example of a website that has three components:

- Payments
- Search
- Reviews

Typically, all of the above components will come under one single architecture. This means that when you access the website, all of the above components are presented to you via a single application. This form of structure is known as a monolithic unit. If you have a monolithic structure, then the more traffic that comes to the website, the more you might need to scale the unit in order to accommodate the traffic.

In the case of a microservice, an application is broken down into various components (in the above example, there are three components to look at). The individual components function as small services that are autonomous.

This means that Payments, Search, and Reviews do not fall under a single application. They each become a separate entity focusing on a single business requirement. They each have their own separate servers but are able to communicate with each other in those instances that they need to rely on each other.

Let us differentiate between a microservice architecture and a monolithic one.

Microservice	Monolithic
Each of the business units of the complete application should be the smallest. It should only be focused on managing one business objective. For example, the Reviews section should only be taking care of allowing users to view, manage, and post reviews.	A single unit that caters to all business objectives.
It is quicker to activate the Service Startup	It takes more time to activate the Service Startup
The microservices are loosely connected to each other. This means that they can rely on each other, but if you perform a change in one, then it won't affect the others.	All the components are coupled tightly. If you make changes in one component, then it could affect the other.
Businesses using this architecture can deploy more resources, based on their objectives and the ROI they wish to achieve.	Businesses cannot allocate resources to individual components. They have to work with the entire architecture or none at all.
Microservices requires small teams. Each team can be responsible for one particular component. This allows you to easily manage the teams. If a particular team is facing a problem or requires assistance, then you can easily understand	A large team is required to manage a monolithic architecture. This means that you need to be able to manage a large team with a large number of moving parts. Anyone could have taken an action that could

the problem or requirement.	produce a certain result. It is up to you to isolate the cause and reaction.
Your main emphasis would mostly be about the product and not the entire project.	The focus of a monolithic architecture is the entire project.

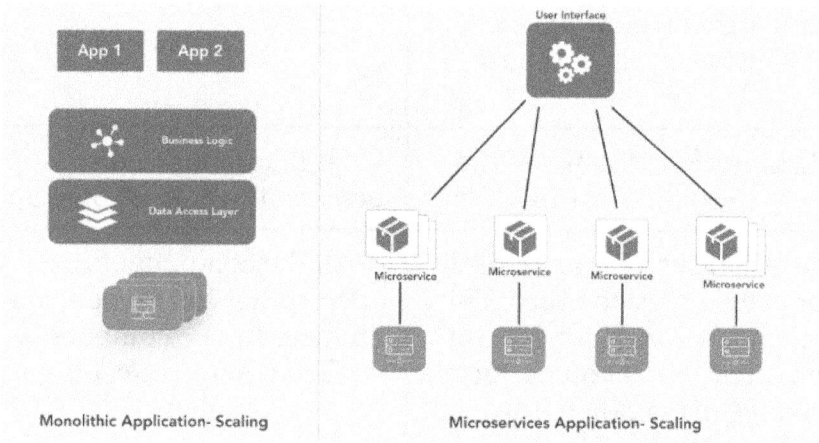

Each component that the user interacts with is a different microservice.

Why Do People Use This Architecture?

You might have spotted a few advantages of working with a microservice as you were looking at the differences between it and a monolithic service. But what exactly makes a microservice stand out?

An important advantage is that you can build a software based on the microservice architecture and you can break it down into multiple components, which allows you greater ease in deploying and redeploying each component. In a monolithic service, redeploying the entire architecture takes a considerable amount of time. Furthermore, when you deploy a particular component, you do not compromise the integrity of the entire structure. You are only going to change the individual component.

Let us suppose that one microservice fails. Using the example above, we focused on three components: **Search**, **Payments**, and **Reviews**. If the Payments component fails, then users can still use the Search and Reviews section. You might have seen this happen when visiting certain websites. You are browsing through the website. You click on a particular section and you are directed towards an error page. You start to look through other sections and realize that they are working perfectly well. This happens because the application is using a microservice architecture. They might be updating the section that was not working well or adding an update to it.

Microservices works well with other containers.

Let us suppose that you have an idea for a particular component. You would really like to implement this idea. It could be an aesthetic change or something more functional. When you decide to implement it, you can do so without disruption in any of the other services. This becomes important when you are planning to change only one section in order to accommodate a certain goal. For example, if you have gone to Amazon, then they are able to easily process discount coupons in the Checkout section. Some of these discounts can be automatic, depending on the time of the year or for a special promotion. But you might notice them for a certain duration and then they are not available anymore. This little change can be easily done because of a microservice structure. What's more, you will have a small team taking care of the changes. This means that you can work with them alone, instead of involving each and every person in the development team.

You can easily monitor the security of each of the components. If you are using a monolithic structure, then when a security breach occurs, you might have to start evaluating various components until you can isolate the problem. In a microservice environment, you can easily see which component has been affected. You simply have to isolate that component, allow other parts to function normally, and easily deal with the problem at hand. This process gives you the opportunity to see security flaws in various parts of your application. Once you realize a vulnerability, you can also send a security update quickly to that component alone. The whole process of discovering the problem, evaluating it, fixing it, and then updating the security of the component can be done quickly because you know where to focus your attention.

Understanding DevOps

One of the best ways to explain DevOps is by taking an example.

Meet Mark.

Mark works for a company whose success depends on the fact that it can offer new and exciting products to its customer base faster than the competitors. Mark's role in the company is that of a developer. This means that he works on writing codes for new products, features, bug fixes, and security updates. However, Mark faces one big problem. He needs to wait weeks before any of the ideas that he has created are implemented into the system. This creates delays, which in turn affects Mark's work. He is unable to bring out updates faster than the competitors. Essentially, Mark is using the traditional system of working (the waterfall method), which is both time-consuming and does not yield the proper results.

He then decides to take a new approach. Rather than focus on all the activities that he has to do, from coding new products to features, he decides to make use of Kubernetes. In the Kubernetes platform, he then splits each piece of the work that he is doing into separate components. The main goal is to create an Automated Delivery (AD) system. This allows Mark to work on each component faster.

Hold on—I still don't see a definition for DevOps. Is it a kind of software?

Now that is where people usually misunderstand DevOps; it is not software. At least, not on its own.

DevOps is a compilation of various practices, policies, and tools that streamlines work in such a manner that avoids delays and allows developers to achieve goals faster.

When someone says that he works as a DevOps engineer or in DevOps, he is not referring to a particular software or program. He is mentioning a set of principles that pays close attention to constant integration, configuration management, and various standardization and automation principles. What this all means is that Mark will be able to put some of his tasks into automation, especially those that don't require his attention each and every time.

Let's take a simple example to explain the above scenario. Assume that you are using MS Word. Imagine that every time you opened it, MS Word does not show a blank page. Instead, it just shows a dialog box and you have to manually click on the File drop-down menu and then choose a New Blank Document. Isn't that rather cumbersome? But that is not the case, is it? Whenever you open MS Word, the software boots up with a blank document on display. Whether you choose to use that blank doc is up to you.

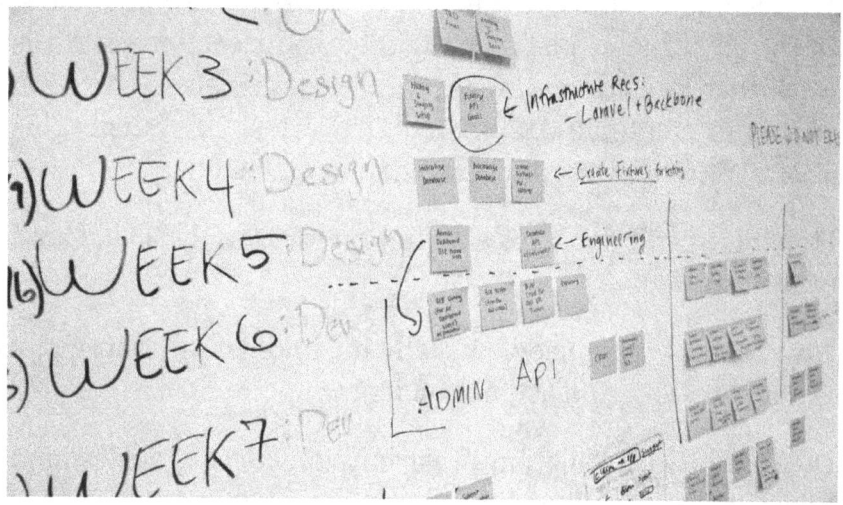

When you use DevOps, you arrange your work in a proper structure.

In DevOps, tasks that can be automated are done so in order to save time. This allows the developer, such as our good friend Mark here, to focus on those components that truly require attention. Even in such cases, if he believes that he can automate most of the component, he can choose to do so.

The result is that he is beating the competition and getting a big fat bonus from his boss (and maybe a corner office with a nice view in the future).

There are two terms to understand in DevOps and they are represented as "AD/CD." And no, that is not the name of a knock-off heavy metal band.

We have already seen what AD refers to, which is Automated Delivery. CD, on the other hand, refers to Continuous Delivery. This means that certain tasks have to be completed over and over again. In the case of Mark, if there are tasks that he needs to do repeatedly, then it would truly be a waste of his time if he has to work on them each and every time. Why not just allow a system to keep performing it without any delay?

If you would like to visualize DevOps, you can think of it as a conveyor belt. Along the belt, there are numerous checks and balances that ensure that the result that comes out at the end of the belt is of high quality. If the result is not good enough, then it is removed from the belt. These checks and balances are the automations that we were talking about, commands that are automatically deployed when the program reaches a certain stage.

However, DevOps is not just about improving the speed. It is also about being proactive. Teams get together to have an awareness about the infrastructure and make sure to put that awareness into action beforehand rather than while the process is taking place.

Let us take the example of a large factory that makes cars. If you already have an awareness about the various parts of cars, then you will install machines in your factory that can automatically perform certain tasks, such as adding doors or fixing wheels. You will be producing faster cars and making sure that the quality meets the standards.

You might then ask the question, What if I want to add another process in order to make things even faster or smoother? You can do that.

In the example above, you can install another machine that takes care of fixing headlights. The trick is to do it in a way that does not slow down the overall process. The same situation applies in software and application development.

You can add in certain components that can help streamline the process. The idea is to make sure that you reduce time wastage as much as possible.

To many people, DevOps can be rather intimidating. But it does not have to be so. The trick is to work with it slowly. For example, using Kubernetes is one step in the DevOps process. You are utilizing an application that greatly improves and speeds the application development process. By simply adding Kubernetes, you have adopted DevOps. Another way DevOps can be utilized is by having one person manage one component. If an application has multiple working parts, then it might not be wise to place the responsibility of their management on one person. Having more people work on the application not only allows you to have different expertise and skills working on the application, but it also gives you the opportunity to easily detect problems and errors.

DevOps and Microservices

Even though microservices makes your job easier, it is still a large amount of work to deal with. Without order and structure, you are not going to be able to deal with the components of microservices.

This is where DevOps comes into play. In fact, DevOps is not just used for microservices, but for other areas of Kubernetes as well.

When you follow the principles of DevOps, you are making work easier for you.

Chapter 3: Understanding Containers

We have looked at how we can get started with Kubernetes. We have even understood how to work effectively with Kubernetes using DevOps.

Finally, we are going to narrow our attention to containers.

We have already understood what containers are. Typically, when you start working with containers, this is the end result.

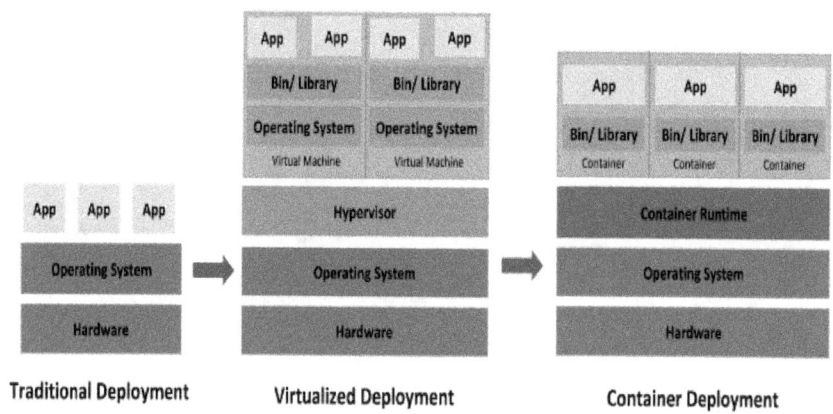

What it looks like working with containers.

Of course, the above diagram shows us an advanced stage of container handling. However, it is good to have an idea of what you can expect with containers.

Working With Fundamentals

Whenever you choose to run an application, it takes up valuable time in your CPU. It also consumes memory space, transmits packages, writes to a certain disk, and even tries to access other devices. If it performs any of the aforementioned tasks, then it consumes resources. The problem with that is the resources are all shared by the same host. Containers allow you to isolate the programs and resources into separate boxes.

Containers come packed with various building blocks, but the two that we need to focus on heavily are cgroups and namespaces.

When you enter the below command for *ps axf*, then you will see a list of processes.

Command string: *$ ps axf*

PID	TTY	STAT	TIME	COMMAND
2	?	S	0:00	[kthreadd]
3	?	S	0:42	_ [ksoftirqd/0]
5	?	S<	0:00	_ [kworker/0:0H]
7	?	S	8:14	_ [rcu_sched]
8	?	S	0:00	_ [rcu_bh]

Source: (Baier, 2017)

If you would like to create a new namespace, then you have to utilize *unshare*. Use the below command:

$ sudo unshare --fork --pid --mount-proc=/proc /bin/sh

$ ps axf

The result will be:

PID   TTY   STAT TIME COMMAND

1   pts/0 S   0:00   /bin/sh

2   pts/0 R+   0:00   ps axf

When you enter the above command, you have created a new pid container.

In order to make things even more clear to you, there are several processes running inside a container. Each of them has a particular PID associated with them.

When you know the pid, then you can isolate the processes. This allows each process to be independent of another. When you can make each one independent, then you can assign resource limits and usage restrictions on each pid. If you don't, then there are chances that one process could consume too much of your device's resources. For example, it could eat up memory to such a degree that you might not have any memory left for other processes. This could cause your device to crash.

Now that you have discovered the pids, how can you set resource limits? In order to do so, you use the cgroups function.

To understand cgroups, we need to continue from the pid namespace that we just looked at. Enter the command: *yes > /dev/null.*

$ yes > /dev/null & top

$	PID	USER	PR	NI	VIRT	RES	SHR	S
	%CPU		%MEM					

| TIME+ | COMMAND |

3	root	20	0	6012	656	584	R
	100.0		0.		0		

| 0:15.15 | yes |

1	root	20	0	4508	708	632	S	0.0
		0.		0				

| 0:00.00 | sh |

| 4 | root | 20 |

Source: (Baier, 2017)

In the above example, the load on your CPU has reached 100% (as noticed by the part that has been highlighted in bold). This is not good since you need to free up some memory to work on other tasks. If you are working on one of the latest iterations of Windows, then you simply have to hit CTRL+ALT+DELETE to bring up the Task Manager (or bring up the Task Manager in your Mac, if you are using it). Once you open the Task Manager, then you will be able to see the CPU usage. If it reaches 100%, then it is usually highlighted in red, indicating that your CPU is incapable of handling any more tasks. Try to push your CPU beyond this point and you might just find out that all the processes you are working on have stalled. The result is a situation that you might call "frozen."

Let's see how you can put a limit on what saps your CPU's capabilities. Use this command: */sys/fs/cgroup/*

```
$ ls /sys/fs/cgroup
```

blkio	cpuset	memory	perf_event
cpu	devices	net_cls	pids
cpuacct	freezer	net_cls,net_prio	systemd
cpu,cpuacct	hugetlb	net_prio	

Source: (Baier, 2017)

Each of the above directories are able to tell you what resources they manage.

Once you have used the list above, then you simply have to use the below command:

$ ps x | grep yes

11809 pts/2 R 12:37 yes

*$ mkdir /sys/fs/cgroup/cpu/box && *

echo 11809 > /sys/fs/cgroup/cpu/box/tasks

And with that, you have added a limit on the CPU usage. Once the limit has been added, applications cannot go past a particular point.

The above steps are just a simple way to get started with containers. Before you can delve into each process, making sure that they are not consuming too much resources is the right way to go.

Starting With Containers

Remember Docker? Well, we are going to start working with it right now.

Just to let you know, Docker isn't the only container engine that you can use. There are others, such as *rkt*. But we are going to be using Docker because it allows us to easily manage, pack, and distribute applications within specific containers.

But is that all there is to Docker? Those are not good reasons to adopt something without question.

I agree. Which is why we are going to quickly go through the benefits of using Docker.

The main advantage of Docker is that it provides a great ROI. It allows you to reduce infrastructure resources drastically, utilizing fewer resources to run similar applications.

Docker allows you to repeat a certain environment. If you have a large team, then this process increases productivity. No longer does each team have to work on something from the ground up. Replicate the environment and the team is good to go.

Another important feature is that Docker is compatible with numerous machines. No more will you worry if the application can run on your machine or not. You can use any laptop or server, and Docker can easily adapt to the environment.

You can deploy Docker in mere seconds. There are no lengthy bootup processes for you to work with.

Let's start by getting Docker ready for your system.

Installing Docker

The first step to note is that you have to ensure that you have *apt* repositories. If you do not have them, then you can get them by using:

$ sudo apt-get install apt-transport-https ca-certificates curl software-properties-common

Next, you have to add in the gpg key. Use:

$ curl -fsSL https://download.docker.com/linux/ubuntu/gpg | sudo apt-key add -

$ sudo apt-key fingerprint 0EBFCD88

The repository should then be set up using *amd64*:

$ sudo add-apt-repository "deb [arch=amd64]

Check for any required updates and if there are, update the package. Use the command:

$ sudo apt-get update

$ sudo apt-get install docker-ce

When you have installed Docker, you can then move on to Dockerfile.

How To Use Dockerfile

Notice that we have been talking about images throughout this book. You might already be aware of this concept, but a refresher on the concept won't hurt. You can think of images as the building blocks of a container. When you start Docker, each container within a pod has a Docker image attached to it. This allows you to easily configure files within the container. Each image is a particular app that is used in the software.

A Dockerfile is a text document that features all the important commands that a user can utilize in order to assemble an image.

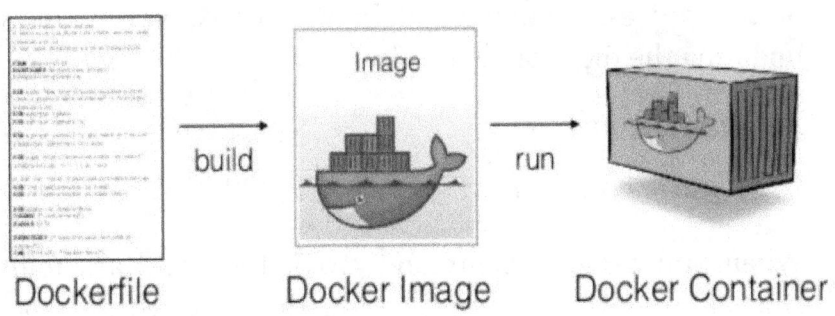

Dockerfile is used to build an image and then run that as a container.

One of the key things to understand is your project structure. It will look something like the below:

app

Dockerfile

requirements.txt

app_folder

file

file

Now you have to think of the app that you would like to use. Let us assume that you are using ubuntu as your base image. In that case, you use:

FROM ubuntu

MAINTAINER   Name   of   the   User <email@emailserver.com>

You have started your Dockerfile. Just like we did with most of the processes mentioned in this book, you begin by updating the file. You do this by:

RUN apt-get update

RUN apt-get upgrade -y

When you use the command RUN, then you are telling Docker to start something within the shell. In the above commands, you are asking Docker to commit an update command.

Once you have executed the RUN command, you then have to move the application into the container. To do that, you have to use the following:

RUN mkdir -p /hostapp

WORKDIR /hostapp

COPY

In the above commands, the "hostapp" refers to the app that you would like to move. The COPY command takes care of the processes. You are now free to run the app. If you would like to, then you simply have to use the following command:

docker build -t myapp

Working With Multiple Containers

Here comes the tricky part. We have understood how to start containers individually. But what if we want to connect one container to another. In fact, what if we would like all the containers to be interconnected? What we do is first create a bridge network, after which we can run all the contents within that network.

In order to create a bridge network, use a command that looks like the below:

$ docker network create kiosk

*$ docker run -d -p 5000:5000 *

-e REDIS_HOST=lcredis --network=kiosk kiosk-example

$ docker run -d --network-alias lcredis --network=kiosk redis

*$ docker run -d -e REDIS_HOST=lcredis -e MYSQL_HOST=lmysql *

*-e   MYSQL_ROOT_PASSWORD=$MYPS   -e MYSQL_USER=root *

--network=kiosk recorder-example

*$ docker run -d --network-alias lmysql -e MYSQL_ROOT_PASSWORD=$MYPS *

--network=kiosk mysql:5.7

Source: (Baier, 2017)

Next, we make use of Docker Compose.

Docker Compose is a useful tool that allows you to work with multiple containers without any problems. Here is an example output that you can create:

docker-compose.yml

Once done, you can use the below command to boot it up:

docker-compose up

You should then see something like this:

$ docker-compose up

Creating network "cwd_default" with the default driver

Creating cwd_hello-world_1

Attaching to cwd_hello-world_1

hello-world_1 |

hello-world_1 | Hello from Docker!

hello-world_1 | This message shows that your installation appears to be working correctly.

...

cwd_hello-world_1 exited with code 0

A typical Docker Compose looks like this:

version: '3'

services:

  web:

    build: .

    ports:

    - "5000:5000"

    volumes:

    - .:/code

    - logvolume01:/var/log

    links:

    - redis

  redis:

    image: redis

volumes:

  logvolume01: {}

Source: (Baier, 2017)

You can then use the above template to create and define the connections.

Chapter 4: Storage and Resources

Kubernetes and Docker both use the disk of the local host. This is a function that appears by default. Docker can then utilize the disk to store and load any data that it wants to. As long as the host is able to maintain sufficient disk space, ensure that the right privileges and permissions are set, and the containers exist, then the data will also exist.

This means that if the host closes the container, then the application crashes after exiting. The container becomes reassigned to another user or host, and whatever data the host was working on will be lost.

To get a better understanding of the above, it is important to look at Kubernetes with respect to volume.

Kubernetes and Volume

Nobody wants to have their data lost, especially when the container becomes terminated. But what can one do?

This is where Volume comes into play.

A Volume is simply a directory on your local disk or within the container. Some of the volumes have data in them, but at its core, it functions as a directory. What kind of directory you create, the kind of medium that supports your directory, and the contents of that directory all depend on the type of volume that you use.

There are many types of volumes. Here are just some of them:

awsElasticBlockStore

cephfs

cinder

azureDisk

downwardAPI

emptyDir

fc (fibre channel)

configMap

csi

azureFile

Each of the above volumes have their own features and capabilities. If you are using the awsElasticBlockStore volume, then you are making use of the services provided by Amazon.

Step 1 of 2

Country

United States	▼

Terms of Service

☐ I have read and agree to the Google Cloud Platform Free Trial Terms of Service.

Required to continue

CONTINUE

It is quite easy to get started on Persistent Disk with Google. Just make sure that you select the proper country.

Since we are using GCE, we are going to make use of the gcePersistentDisk volume. This volume offers something called the Persistent Disk.

Essentially, it is a form of storage option that is provided by Google. By default, each GCE comes with a Persistent Disk. However, if you would like to add more in case you would like more storage or better options for the storage, then you can head over to *https://cloud.google.com/compute/docs/disks/* and look at what Google has to offer.

In order to make use of a Persistent Disk (PD), you need to first create it. Use the below command:

gcloud compute disks create --size=xxxGB --zone=myzone my-data-disk

You have to mention the size based on the total size that is available to you. For example, some PDs that are offered by Google come with nearly 1TB of space. If you have that much space, then you can assign a value to the size. Here is an example:

gcloud compute disks create --size=700GB --zone=myzone my-data-disk

What you have done is utilize only 700 of the 1,000 GB space allotted to you. The "zone" part refers to the zone that you reside in. If you are in the US, then you have to input "us-central1-a." When you do, it should look like:

gcloud compute disks create --size=xxxGB --zone=us-central1-a my-data-disk

Now let us say that you would like to utilize the entire space available to you and you are within the US. Your command should look something like this:

gcloud compute disks create --size=1,000GB --zone=us-central1-a my-data-disk

With that, you can execute your command and you have created a volume.

Your next step would be to use a PD with a pod. Here Is a sample command:

```
apiVersion: yourversion
kind: Pod
metadata:
  name: test-pd
spec:
  containers:
  - image: k8s.gcr.io/test-webserver
    name: test-container
    volumeMounts:
    - mountPath: /test-pd
      name: test-volume
  volumes:
  - name: test-volume
    # This GCE PD must already exist.
    gcePersistentDisk:
      pdName: my-data-disk
      fsType: ext4
```

Source: (Baier, 2017)

The pod that you are using will have its own details. Make sure that you use those details for the PD you are creating. If you would like to know more details about a particular component, then you can use the below commands:

kubectl get services: List all services in the namespace

kubectl get pods --all-namespaces: List all pods in all namespaces

kubectl get deployment my-dep: List a particular deployment

Functionalities of Kubernetes Volumes

You can think of a volume as a directory that is accessible by the containers in a pod. There are various types of volumes and the type that you choose helps you determine how the volume is created and its content and functions.

We had already listed some of these volumes above, but we did not take an in-depth look at some of the important ones. Here are the popular Kubernetes volumes that are widely used:

emptyDir

This type of volume is initially created when the node gets attached to a pod. This volume remains in function for as long as the pod is active. In the beginning, the volume is empty and the pod can use the directory within emptyDir to read and write. Once you separate the pod from the node, then the data that you were working on within the emptyDir is deleted.

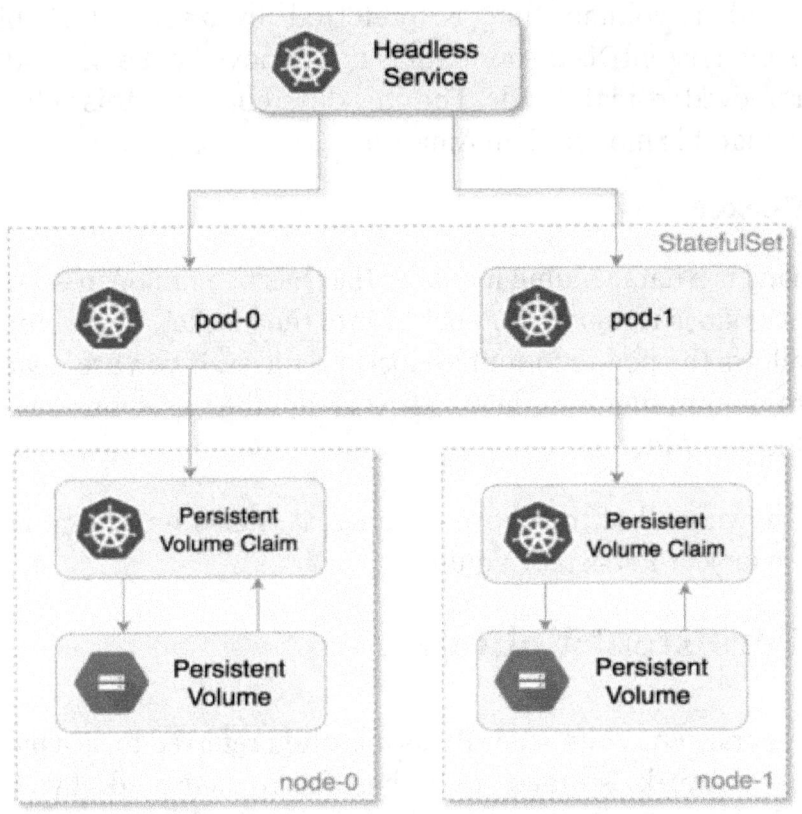

Under each pod, you will find a volume.

gcePersistentDisk

In this type of volume, a GCE Persistent Disk is mounted on the pod. All the data used in the gcePersistentDisk does not get deleted when the pod is separated from the node. Because of this level of data integrity, users often choose the gcePersistentDisk.

awsElasticBlockStore

Another volume that is preferred by users. Just like gcePersistentDisk, your data is not removed once the pod is removed from the node. The only difference with this volume is that it is mounted on Amazon.

flocker

This is a data volume manager that has been in open-source ever since it was first launched into the market. This volume allows the pod to mount a Flocker dataset. If you are unable to mount, then you have to first create the dataset using the Flocker API.

Knowing all of the above volumes, it is also important that we look at Persistent Volume.

Persistent Volume

A Persistent Volume, or PV as it is often referred to, is a piece of network storage that has been activated by the administrator. It is a particular resource in the cluster.

It's a piece of network storage that has been provisioned by the administrator. It's a resource in the cluster which is independent of any individual pod that uses the PV.

So far in the book, we have looked at workloads that we could start and stop whenever we wanted without any problems. When you are actually working with applications in the real world, then you will be working with data that you do not want to lose. We have already seen that when the container dies, so does the data. However, we can use volumes in order to protect our data and ensure that it does not simply disappear when we make changes to the container. By using a volume, you will be creating a storage space within your own server or machine. Using a volume works well when you have full control of the cluster.

But when it comes to working on a large scale, then the developers would rather choose to use storage that is managed separately. In other words, they make use of an external server. This allows them to remove the focus on storage and then put all their attention on the application or software development itself.

Let's take an example of using MS Word. You enter certain data and you have to manually save the file. Let's say that the power goes out in your house or building. All the data that you have been working on is lost, unless you have manually saved your data. But if you are using Google Docs, then you do not have to worry about losing data. This is because you are saving your file on the Google server. This way, every time you work, your data is saved automatically and even if something were to happen, your data is not affected by the situation.

This is the same with Persistent Volume. But in order to make this happen, we need to find some way for the application to request and specify the storage without being affected by how the storage is provided. In short, Persistent Volumes are similar to volumes, with the only difference being that they are provided by the administrator of the cluster and are independent of a specific pod. The developer or user can then claim the volume by using the Persistent volume Claim function.

Let us go back to GCE and find out how we can create a Persistent Disk.

Step 1

Head over to the console. You should be able to find this in the Compute Engine section. Navigate to Disks. You will be presented with a new screen on which you will spot the Create Disk option. Click the option.

Step 2

You will be given an option to choose a name for the volume. Enter the name that you prefer and then add a brief description of the volume in the space provided. Make sure that the description is something that you recognize, on the off chance that you would like to refer to it in the future. There is a drop-down menu where you can choose the zone. Remember this: you can only choose the Zone that is the same as your nodes within the cluster. GCE PDs cannot be attached to modes and machines in different zones.

Step 3

In the name field, enter *mysite-volume-1*. In the section marked Source Type, choose None (blank disk). For the Size value, enter 10 GB. Do not worry too much about the size for now. We will start with 10 GB and once you are used to the feature, you can begin working with a value that fits your purpose.

GCE allows us to mount more than one node. However, we are going to start by mounting our volume to one pod. Use the below parameters in order to mount the volume.

apiVersion: v1

kind: Pod

```
metadata:

name: test-gce

spec:

containers:

- image: nginx:latest

ports:

- containerPort: 80

name: test-gce

volumeMounts:

- mountPath: /usr/share/nginx/html

name: gce-pd

volumes:

- name: gce-pd

gcePersistentDisk:

pdName: mysite-volume-1

fsType: ext4
```

Source: (Baier, 2017)

Our next step is to use the create command to form the node and then use the describe command in order to discover which node is being used. Simply use:

$ kubectl create -f storage-gce.yaml

$ kubectl describe pod/test-gce

A list of details will display. The most important among them is the IP address. Make sure that you note them both.

Boot up the SSH session.

Now enter the following command:

$ gcloud compute --project "<Your project ID>" ssh --zone "<your gce zone>" "<Node running test-gce pod>"

We have already viewed the volume while the container has been running. We are now able to access it using the node. However, we do need to understand where the node is mounted. So use the below command to transfer to root:

$ sudo su -

$ df -h | grep mysite-volume-1

We have now confirmed one thing—the node is being used for the GCE mount. This makes things easier for us. Earlier, we noticed the mount path listed in the df command. Use that to change the particular folder. To do so, we need to create a new folder:

$ cd   /var/lib/kubelet/plugins/kubernetes.io/gce-pd/mounts/mysite-volume-1

$ vi index.html

Now enter a simple message such as "Hello this is GCE PD!" or you can enter something that you like. You can do this by using your favorite editor. Save your file and then exit from the editor you are using.

If you have followed the above steps correctly, you should see the message that you typed. When you are working with it on your application, then you can use that volume for central storage or your entire website.

At this point, we need to create a Replication Controller, or RC. An RC is a simple function that helps you manage pods. If there are extra pods consuming resources, then RC will remove some of those pods. If there are too few pods, then the RC will create additional pods. But why do we need an RC? Can't we remove and add pods by ourselves? You can, but making the whole process automated is highly convenient. Besides, imagine yourself working on a project or software. You are in the middle of a sensitive task when you realize that you have to start managing your pods. Wouldn't that be highly inconvenient for you to stop what you are doing, lose your train of thought and destroy the process you were working on simply to add or remove pods. When you use an RC, you are allowing the program to automatically delete, terminate, or replace pods when they fail or if the need arises.

For example, let us say that you were performing routine maintenance on your system. During the maintenance, one of your pods failed. Your current situation would entail that you wait for the maintenance to be completed before you can finally work on the pod. But in the case of an RC, it immediately identifies the pod and replaces it easily.

We are going to learn how you can create an RC that is capable of running three web servers that are all running on your PD.

You need to first run the below configuration:

```
apiVersion: v1

kind: ReplicationController

metadata:

name: http-pd

labels:

name: http-pd

spec:

replicas: 3

selector:

name: http-pd

template:

metadata:

name: http-pd

labels:

name: http-pd

spec:

containers:

- image: nginx:latest

- containerPort: 80

name: http-pd
```

volumeMounts:

- mountPath: /usr/share/nginx/html

name: gce-pd

volumes:

- name: gce-pd

gcePersistentDisk:

pdName: mysite-volume-1

fsType: ext4

readOnly: true

Your next resource would be to create an external service. This makes things easier for us when we simply want to view the RC.

apiVersion: v1

kind: Service

metadata:

name: http-pd

labels:

name: http-pd

spec:

type: LoadBalancer

ports:

- name: http

protocol: TCP

port: 80

selector:

name: http-pd

Source: (Baier, 2017)

Once you have created the above resources, then you are ready to go. You might need to wait for a few moments in order for the external IP to be assigned. If you would like to see this external IP, then all you need to do is use the describe command:

$ kubectl describe service/http-pd

Resource Management

We have already talked a bit about resources. Essentially, when you create a pod, you can specify how much RAM and CPU each container requires. When you specify resources to containers, then the platform can make better decisions about which nodes to use for which pods.

The most important resource types that you are aware of are RAM and CPU, memory and space. Each of these resources that you are going to use has a base unit. The base unit of *memory* is represented by bytes and that of *CPU* uses the term cores.

How do resources work exactly?

When you first create a pod, then the Kubernetes scheduler becomes activated. A scheduler is an important component of Kubernetes that is responsible for controlling performance and managing capacity.

When the scheduler first becomes activated, it selects a node for the pod that you have created. Each node has a specific capacity that consists of each of the resource types that we had mentioned earlier: memory and CPU. The scheduler's job is to ensure that when using the resources, the sum of the resources is maintained within the capacity of the node. In other words, the combined resources of memory and CPU should not exceed the capacity of the pod. If it goes beyond the capacity, then the system might crash or the application might fail.

In order to manage your resources, the first step is to create a namespace. You can do this by using the following command:

kubectl create namespace default-mem-example

Your next step is to create a LimitRange. A limit range is just what the name says. It creates a certain limit on the resources that are used by the pod or container within a namespace. You will need a configuration file for the LimitRange. You can use the below:

apiVersion: v1

kind: LimitRange

metadata:

  name: mem-limit-range

```
spec:

 limits:

 - default:

   memory: 512Mi

  defaultRequest:

   memory: 256Mi

  type: Container
```

Source: (Baier, 2017)

If you create a container at this moment, then you might usually have to mention the memory and resource limit. If you do not, then by default, a memory limit of 512MB is applied and a memory request of 256MB is provided.

This ensures that all resources are maintained within the limit that you have specified.

While it is important to mention the limit of the resources, we should also make sure that there is continuous delivery of functions. How can we do that? Let us take a look.

Chapter 5: Continuous Delivery

Once you set up Kubernetes and start working with containers, you are going to face your next challenge—just how are you going to keep your work going continuously? For that, we have *continuous delivery*.

The function of continuous delivery is just what the name suggests; it ensures that there is no interruption in the services that you are providing. This feature allows you to deliver all the latest features and updates without having to stop the service.

Continuous Integration or Continuous Delivery (abbreviated by CI or CD) requires ephemeral builds. An ephemeral build is a fancy name that is given to a process where you create a fresh environment for each build that you are working on. Once you have finished the steps in a build, then you can destroy the build and move on to the next one. Docker is perfect for this task. This is because you can easily create containers in a few seconds and remove them after you have finished your tasks with a build.

Updating Kubernetes Resources

One thing that you can do with Kubernetes is ensure that you keep the updates rolling. For this purpose, you utilize a feature known as the rolling update. This feature updates an application, whether you would like to change it to a new version or change some of its constituent parts, in a continuous manner. Rolling updates also ensure that one instance is updated at any given time. If you were to start updating all the instances simultaneously, then your application might crash or encounter a downtime. At the same time, when you use a rolling update, then you can easily spot any errors. This allows you to rollback to a previous version, fix the errors, and allow a fresh update to happen.

For example, let's say that you are launching a visual update of your application. The update is underway, after which you are going to launch another update that focuses on a specific feature. So far, so good. While the update is underway, you notice that some of the visual features do not look the way you would like them to be. Perhaps the design creates a visual overload or perhaps the colors do not go well together. Whatever the reason, you can stop the update and then rollback in order to focus on the aesthetics. If, for example, you were updating both the visuals and the features at the same time, you won't be able to easily spot the error. In a real-life scenario, you are not going to be working on just two aspects of your application; updates usually have more than two components, from the visual aspects to the features to security and lots more. When you are simultaneously updating them, you might fail to spot a problem before the update has been fully launched.

In order to enable continuous delivery, you will need the help of certain tools. There are many tools that you can utilize for this purpose and they can help with setting up your delivery pipelines.

Let us examine one of them, Gulp.

Gulp.js

The single greatest benefit of using Gulp.js is that it provides a framework to use different builds. Each build can be formed in a code. Because the process is in a code form, you can easily refine your process. The best way to see this process in action is by using an example. We are going to see how to complete a workflow by converting a Docker image to the final Kubernetes result.

Getting Started

In order to get started, you need to have certain prerequisites. One of those prerequisites is a NodeJS package. If you do not already have this package, you can easily get it at *https://docs.npmjs.com/getting-started/installing-node.*

Once you have downloaded the package and installed it, you can check whether it is functioning normally by using a simple command: *node -v*

You will also need a DockerHub and Docker CE in order to create a new image. All the necessary instructions can be found at *https://docs.docker.com/installation/.*

You might then have to create a Docker account, which can be easily done at *https://hub.docker.com/.*

You will then be provided with your login credentials. Use those credentials to gain access to your platform through a simple command: *$ docker login.*

Performing a Build

Now we are going to create a build. For this, we are going to use a directory named node-gulp. This is just an example directory. Once you have learned how to work with Gulp you can make your own directories. Use the below commands in order to get started:

$ mkdir node-gulp

$ cd node-gulp

After entering the above commands, the environment will start installing the gulp package. Once the installation is complete, then you have to check whether all the components were installed and are running properly. To do so, use:

$ npm install -g gulp

We should also make sure that you have gulp on your path.

$ gulp -v

After the initial checks, we are going to transfer gulp into our preferred project folder. We will also be installing additional components such as the gulp-shell and gulp-git.

$ npm install --save-dev gulp

$ npm install gulp-git -save

$ npm install --save-dev gulp-shell

We turn our attention to Kubernetes. We need to create a service destination file and then create a controller. You can use the following code for the process:

apiVersion: v1

kind: ReplicationController

```
metadata:

name: node-gulp

labels:

name: node-gulp

spec:

replicas: 1

selector:

name: node-gulp

template:

metadata:

labels:

name: node-gulp

spec:

containers:

- name: node-gulp

image: <your username>/node-gulp:latest

imagePullPolicy: Always

ports:

- containerPort: 80
```

Source: (Baier, 2017)

In our next step, we need to change the username. In its place, we are going to use the username we received from Docker. Refer to the following code for how to do it:

```
apiVersion: v1

kind: Service

metadata:

name: node-gulp

labels:

name: node-gulp

spec:

type: LoadBalancer

ports:

- name: http

protocol: TCP

port: 80

selector:

name: node-gulp
```

Let's start with a simple task. Simply take the pod that we are working on and create a load balancer. Refer to the code below to understand how this is done:

```
var gulp = require('gulp');

var git = require('gulp-git');
```

```
var shell = require('gulp-shell');

// Clone a remote repo

gulp.task('clone', function(){

return

git.clone('https://github.com/jonbaierCTP/getting-
started-with-kubernetes-se.git', function (err) {

if (err) throw err;

});

});

// Update codebase

gulp.task('pull', function(){

return git.pull('origin', 'master', {cwd: './getting-started-
with-kubernetes-

se'}, function (err) {

if (err) throw err;

});

});

//Build Docker Image

gulp.task('docker-build', shell.task([

'docker build -t <your username>/node-gulp ./getting-
started-with
```

kubernetes-se/docker-image-source/container-info/',

'docker push <your username>/node-gulp'

]));

//Run New Pod

gulp.task('create-kube-pod', shell.task([

'kubectl create -f node-gulp-controller.yaml',

'kubectl create -f node-gulp-service.yaml'

]));

//Update Pod

gulp.task('update-kube-pod', shell.task([

'kubectl delete -f node-gulp-controller.yaml',

'kubectl create -f node-gulp-controller.yaml'

]));

Source: (Baier, 2017)

And with that, you are done. Now your final task is to make sure that you have the gulpfile.js. Within this file, you can easily define your builds.

When you open the file, you might be bombarded with a lot of options. The ones we need to focus on are the following:

create-kube-pod: This allows us to create the service and the controller for the first time.

update-kube-pod: This function allows us to replace an existing controller.

Since this is your first time, you simply have to execute the below command:

$ gulp create-kube-pod

With that, you are done. At this point, you can use the kubectl command to get the IP address for the service that we have started.

When you launch future updates, you can use the below command:

$ gulp pull

$ gulp docker-build

$ gulp update-kube-pod

Improving Kubernetes Deployment

There are many tools at your disposal to greatly improve application deployment using Kubernetes. Right now, I am going to show you a few best practices that you can use to improve the deployment.

Using Authorized Images

Do not add any old image that you come across. You cannot simply trust each and every app that you spot. You need to properly understand the images you are downloading.

If you start running an image that does not adhere to the policies set up by your organization, then there are chances that you might start running malicious or even vulnerable containers.

The best way to explain this is by taking the example of an app that you download from the Android or iOS App store. Most of the trusted apps are easy to download. However, certain apps require you to specifically allow your device to give permission to unknown applications to function within your device.

The same scenario applies with images. If you download and run images from unknown sources, then it could be dangerous. Try not to do that unless you are absolutely certain about the program you are running.

You can create a separate registry where you can store all your images. Make sure that only approved images are used within these registries.

Since Kubernetes uses images that go into a node, only use those images that you trust.

Access Limits

Do not give SSH access to everyone that you know. Keep it limited to only important personnel. This reduces the risk of an unauthorized entry into the resource.

But what if you would like teams or individuals to work on the container? In that case, you can make use of the kubectl exec command. This command allows users to access the container but not gain entry into the host resource.

You can even use the Kubernetes Authorization Plugins in order to maintain even more limitations on access. You can fine-tune the responsibilities and features that you allow users to take control of and even mention specific containers that can be used. For example, if you have a container that features codes that you would not like everyone to know, then you can restrict access to that single container while all other containers are open. You can even restrict certain operations that you think could affect the integrity of the project.

Resource Boundaries

Another limitation that you can place is based on the permissions that you give users. This is different from the previous point because in this section, we are talking about access to resources. For example, if a container requires a set amount of resources, then you can place the limitation on resources and prevent anyone from trying to access additional resources. When the need for extra resources comes into play, users won't be able to simply make decisions on their own. They have to approach you and explain the reason for their requirement. Based on the situation, you can decide if you would like to allow extra resources to be pooled into a particular area or not.

You can create resources in one namespace. You can then choose to hide the namespace from other namespaces. In a default setting, each resource that you create runs within a namespace called default. Apart from the default namespace, you can create additional namespaces. For example, let us call the additional namespaces as *namespace 1* and *namespace 2*. Imagine that you are working on default but other users are focusing on *namespace 1* and *namespace 2*. You can create settings where the user focusing on *namespace 1* does not have access to default and *namespace 2*. At the same time, you can even allow certain namespaces to read from another namespace. Let us look at the below example:

{

"apiVersion": "abac.authorization.kubernetes.io/v1beta1",

"kind": "Policy",

```
"spec": {

  "user": "default",

  "namespace": "namespace2",

  "resource": "pods",

  "readonly": true }

}
```

Source: (Baier, 2017)

What you have done is allow default to read from *namespace 2.*

Segment Your Network

In some cases, you might want to make sure that containers are communicating with only those containers that they are supposed to. However, if the network is shared between containers, then there is a certain freedom of communication. This could mean that if one container becomes compromised, then it could attack all the other containers within the same network.

Typically, it is a challenge to segment the network based on pods and containers. This is because of the dynamic characteristics of containers shared on the network. What this means is that container identities are based on IPs and sometimes each container might have its own IP. Hence, segmenting the containers becomes a complicated task.

Thankfully, if you are on the Google Cloud Platform, then you have certain benefits that you can make use of. You can make use of the firewall settings that prevent one cluster from communicating with another cluster.

For example, if you have *cluster1* that features a few containers, then those containers can only communicate with each other. They cannot affect containers in *cluster2*.

Make Sure You Log

When you are working with Kubernetes, you have the ability to log your activity in a central log. This allows you to periodically check the logs to spot any inconsistencies or problems that you might not have spotted when you were running certain processes. We are going to learn more about monitoring and logging in the next couple of chapters.

Chapter 6: Monitoring

In the real world, you are monitoring not just to check if everything is up and running properly. Of course, we have already seen how you can perform health checks in order to discover application problems. However, I truly believe in the old adage that mentions that prevention is always better than the alternative.

In any organization, best practices dictate that teams are able to anticipate problems and deal with them before anything goes online. But this is easier said than done. Despite best efforts, certain problems always creep into the application. However, the fact still remains: you need to reduce problems as much as possible.

But what happens once you have launched the application? What if problems start appearing then?

This is where the process of monitoring comes into play. By monitoring the containers and all other components of the application, including the resources, you are keeping an eye out for any trends or patterns that deviate from normal functions. You need to have a clear view of the containers you are managing, ensuring that their performance and the availability of network, system, and OS functions are taken into account.

We are going to learn various ways to monitor our cluster resources.

Monitoring in Kubernetes

Kubernetes already comes with certain monitoring capabilities. If you would like to take a look at these functions, then you simply have to use the below command:

$ kubectl get pods --namespace=kube-system

With the growth of microservices, monitoring and logging has become even more complex than before. There are so many moving components for you to look at one point. There are also numerous applications, each of them diversified and distributed while also communicating with each other. All these factors make monitoring a more complex task.

Before we move onto the monitoring process, let us look at two ways that you can monitor.

Cluster Monitoring

In this process, your main objective is to monitor the health and condition of one whole cluster in Kubernetes. Some administrators prefer to know if all the nodes within a cluster are working properly, if they are compromised in any manner, and the number of applications that are functioning within each node. They would also like to know the resources consumed by all of these various components.

Monitoring allows you to look at how your clusters are utilizing resources.

Pod Monitoring

When focusing on a pod, the process of monitoring can be categorized into three forms:

- Application metrics
- Container metrics
- Kubernetes metrics

First, let's take a look at application metrics. These are metrics that are created by the application itself and are based on the goals of the organization.

If you are interested in finding out information about a particular container, then you have to utilize container metrics. You will find out more details about memory, CPU, and network usage.

In order to monitor a particular pod and the way its deployment is being handled by users or administrators, you can use Kubernetes metrics. You can gain the following information through these metrics:

- How many instances were expected by the pod and how many does it currently have?

- Is the progress of deployment going smoothly?
- Is there enough network data for the pods and do you need to perform any changes to the network services?

Monitoring Metrics

The method to monitor the various components of your cluster is not complicated. You just need the right tools for the job.

One of the tools that you can use is called DaemonSets. Typically, Kubernetes automatically ensures that each node that whatever you create comes with a DaemonSet pod. If you destroy a node, then the attached DaemonSet pod is also destroyed. This means that for every cluster node, there is a specific DaemonSet for the purpose of monitoring.

You can also make use of Prometheus as your monitoring platform.

Using Prometheus

To work with Prometheus, make sure that you have downloaded and installed the latest version of the file. You can find the file here: *https://prometheus.io/download/*

Once you have the file on your system, you have to extract it. Enter the command below:

tar xvfz prometheus-*.tar.gz

cd prometheus-*

Once the extraction process is complete, then you can start prometheus by using a simple command:

./prometheus --config.file=prometheus.yml

With the program running, you are able to easily start getting the metrics that you want.

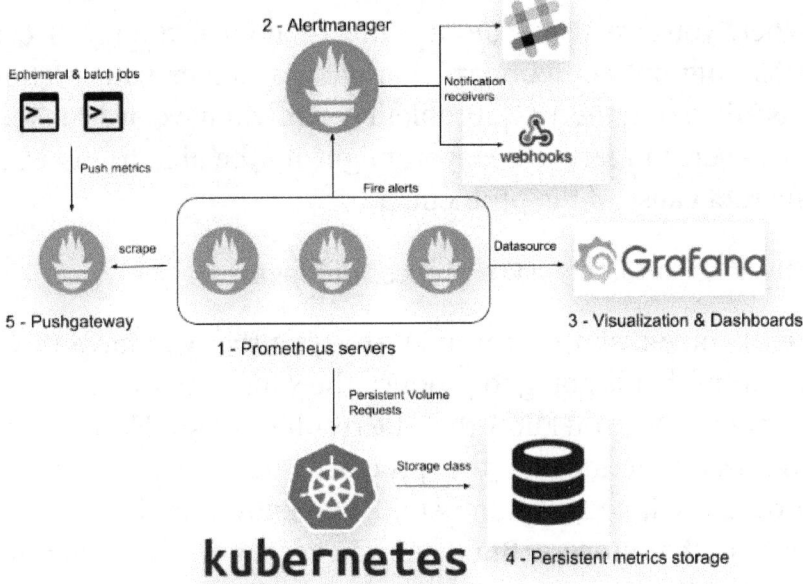

Prometheus allows you to connect with various services all at once.

Chapter 7: Logging

When you are using monitoring functions, then you can easily dig out components that show whether your system has failed or if there is a problem you might have overlooked. However, in many cases, you might not be able to discover the root cause of the problem.

This is why you have the process of logging.

Let us take a simple example. Imagine that you have run a program that is going to produce the sum of all the numbers from 1 to 100. You know that the result is 5,050. However, as you were monitoring the process, you realized that the program skipped the number 50. You know that there was an error in that process. But when you get the result, you notice that the final number is 4,900. You know that the program has omitted the number 50, but you don't know what other numbers were removed and for that matter, why those numbers have been excluded. You then go to the log and notice where the errors have happened and also why they occurred.

The process of logging allows you to refine your program so that it makes fewer and fewer errors in the future. Think of it this way: monitoring allows you to effectively look at the present situation of the program. However, logging allows you go back to the beginning if you would like to and check for any inconsistencies.

Generally, there are two important posts to a logging system. You have the logging agent and then the backend.

The logging agent is a layer that is responsible for gathering information and dispatching the information to the backend. When the information reaches the backend, then all the logs are saved. One of the most challenging parts of creating logs is for Kubernetes to determine how to gather logs from various containers and then transfer them to a centralized backend. Thankfully, there is a solution for that.

The most efficient method of creating logs is to assign logging agents for each and every node and configuring them in such a way that they forward all the information to one destination. To do so, we can create what is known as a sidecar container. A sidecar container is a special utility entity. It does not perform any actions on its own, but actually supports the main container. This process is useful to us, as we can simply create a sidecar container to deal with the logs of each container within a pod. That way, we do not have to worry about managing each and every log file since that is automatically done by the sidecar container. Here is a script that you can use for such a sidecar container:

---6-2_logging-sidecar.yml---

apiVersion: v1

kind: Pod

metadata:

name: myapp

spec:

containers:

- image: busybox

```
name: application
args:
- /bin/sh
- -c
- >
while true; do
echo "$(date) INFO hello" >> /var/log/myapp.log;
sleep 1;
done
volumeMounts:
- name: log
mountPath: /var/log
- name: sidecar
image: busybox
args:
- /bin/sh
- -c
- tail -fn+1 /var/log/myapp.log
volumeMounts:
- name: log
```

mountPath: /var/log

volumes:

- name: log

emptyDir: {}

Source: (Baier, 2017)

With that, you have successfully created your monitoring and logging capabilities within Kubernetes.

However, there is much more to logging, especially when we take into consideration Fluentd and Elasticsearch. Let us look into these two concepts in detail.

Understanding logging is not possible without understanding some of the basic components that comprise logging.

The first component that we need to look at is stdout.

The stdout or standard output is the default file descriptor that is used by a particular process in order to produce an output. A file descriptor refers to a unique number that identifies a particular file in your operating system.

For example, your Word software might have the file descriptor of 12 and MS PowerPoint might have the file descriptor iofg 567. Each program has its own number and this is used by the operating system whenever it would like to access that program or provides its location to another software.

Let's take an example here. You might have heard of the popular file extracting software WinRAR. Your operating system might give WinRAR a file descriptor of 56. Now let's imagine that you have a compressed file that you would like to extract. When you use WinRAR to extract your file, then your OS lets the file know that it should be looking for the program with the file descriptor 56. Think of file descriptors as the number plates on a car; each number lets you know which car you are looking for.

Your individual containers utilize stdout in order to create output. It is this output that we need to be concerned about since it contains all the details of the activity performed by the particular container.

Another component that we need to look at is stderr. This functions similar to stdout, but the main purpose of the stderr is to write error messages.

We now have two different output methods, the stdout and stderr. The easiest way to record logs is to create two sidecar containers for the two methods of recording output, where one method (stdout) handles the activity while the other (stderr) handles the error.

Here is an example of an activity that will result in a container creating a logging entry to stdout:

apiVersion: v1

kind: Pod

metadata:

name: example

spec:

containers:

- name: example

image: busybox

args: [/bin/sh, -c, 'while true; do echo $(date); sleep 1; done']

Source: (Baier, 2017)

In order to check the logs of that container, you simply have to use the log container-name command.

So far, so good. Now we get into the details.

Fluentd

Your biggest problem is not the log itself. After all, we just looked at how you can create a sidecar container to manage your logs. Your biggest challenge is to gather the logs from hundreds of different sources and unify them, a task that is much more complicated than it sounds. If you are a system administrator, then you are going to be constantly dealing with complex sets of procedures to analyze and parse service logs. Add to this the fact that you are not just going to be utilizing applications on a PC or laptop browser, but making sure that the application runs smoothly on mobile devices and you have so many different areas to look at. It reaches a point where it is physically impossible for you to start extracting logs from everywhere.

In such scenarios, you need a platform that provides you the below benefits when it comes to logging:

- The platform is a high-performing one
- There is minimal data loss
- The system is reliable

This is where Fluentd comes into play. Fluentd is a platform that allows you to gather a high-performing layer for your container that allows it to assist you with the logging process.

One of the unique characteristics of Fluentd is that it structures data in such a way that it becomes easy to unify all the various aspects of log data. It can easily collect, filter, buffer, and then create an output for the data logs from multiple sources and components.

In order to install Fluentd, your first step is to download the *msi* file that you can find right here: *https://td-agent-package-browser.herokuapp.com/3/windows*

Once you have installed the *msi* file, you are going to spot this program: *Td-agent Command Prompt*. Activate it by double-clicking the program icon.

In the next step, you will notice a prompt. Enter the below command:

> fluentd -c etc\td-agent\td-agent.conf

Execute the above command and then launch another Td-agent Command Prompt. In the second prompt, you have to type this command:

> echo {"message":"hello"} | fluent-cat test.event

For the next step, we have to make sure that you register the program to your Windows so that it can use your system as a permanent process. In order to do so, run the Td-agent

Command Prompt again. This time, enter the below commands:

> *fluentd --reg-winsvc i*

> *fluentd --reg-winsvc-fluentdopt '-c C:/opt/td-agent/etc/td-agent/td-agent.conf -o C:/opt/td-agent/td-agent.log'*

Source: (Baier, 2017)

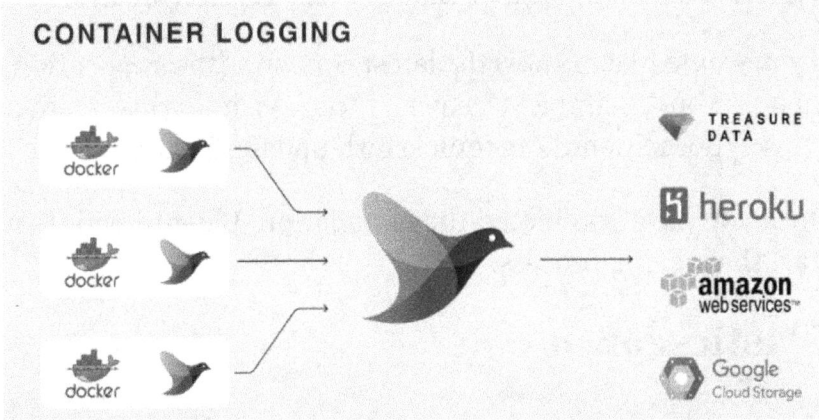

CONTAINER LOGGING

Fluentd takes logs from Docker and then stores them in your chosen cloud service platform such as GCE or AWS.

For the next step, you need to navigate to the Control Panel in the Windows menu. Head over to System and Security. Then you have to navigate to Administrative Tools and finally click on Services.

You will be able to see an option that says Fluentd Window Service. Open the application and then click the option Start. You should be able to see the below at this point, which shows that you have successfully installed the application:

> *net start fluentd winsvc*

The Fluentd Windows Service service is starting.

The Fluentd Windows Service service was started successfully.

For the final step, we are going back to Td-agent Command Prompt. Once you open the prompt, you are going to update the application. Simply enter the below command and you are good to go:

> *fluent-gem install fluent-plugin-xyz --version=XXX*

If you would like to know the latest version of the application, then you simply have to visit this link: https://docs.fluentd.org/quickstart/update-from-v0.12

Once you have completed the installation, Fluentd will then start the logging process.

Elasticsearch

Think about this scenario.

You have compiled large volumes of data. This volume keeps increasing the more logs you create. Imagine that one day, you decide to examine the data because you discovered a problem in your application. Wouldn't that be such a cumbersome job to do now that you have so much data to sift through? You can't possibly go through each and every piece of data hoping to find what you are looking for. Wouldn't it be convenient if you had a search function where you simply have to enter a value and you are taken to that data?

This is where Elasticsearch becomes your preferred tool for search-related functions. Regular database management systems are not meant for performing complex searches or running full-text queries.

In order to use elasticsearch, you do not require a complicated installation procedure. Simple head over to their web page and download the latest version. You can start off with a trial mode and then shift to a full version if you feel like it is something you might use for the long term.

Simply head over to *https://www.elastic.co/downloads/* to find the file and download it onto your system.

While we are adding new components to our database, it is also important to maintain its integrity. This is where the concept of security comes into place.

So how can we secure the various components that we are working with? We shall look at that in the next chapter.

Chapter 8: Network and Security

When you would like to implement networking in Kubernetes, you are spoiled with an array of choices. There really is no particular option that you have to stick to for networking purposes. The only points that you have to keep in mind while networking are:

- All of the containers you are working on should be accessible to each other without the presence of NAT. It does not matter what nodes they are on. The interconnectedness should exist between them. What exactly is NAT? We are going to take a look at it after this segment.
- The nodes should be able to communicate with any container.

The basic idea behind NAT is that it provides a pub address to a device or a group of devices within a private network, such as an organization. But the basic idea might not make sense to many people, so let us use an example.

Imagine that you have about 10 computers in your organization and all of them have access to the public network. This situation means that there are 10 different IP addresses with access to the internet. Now imagine that all 10 users are dealing with sensitive information. In your case, they are all working on your application and you would not like the details of the application to be made public. If one person's computer becomes hacked, then your entire security might become compromised. To solve this problem, all the computers in your network can be connected to a single public network, which in turn is connected to the internet. This means that only one IP address is presented to the internet. If you are the administrator, then you can place restrictions on the address, such as the number of devices that can connect to it, what kind of information they can access, what software or programs are blocked, and so on. All of this gives you the power to control the information that goes to and from the devices in your organization.

Because we are referring to access, we need to talk about ingress.

What Is Ingress?

We briefly touched upon ingress in the introductory chapter. But just what can ingress do and why is this important?

In short, ingress allows access to your Kubernetes components from outside the cluster. In other words, it reveals your HTTP and HTTPS to the services that you have within your Kubernetes.

As you can see, this could be quite dangerous at times, as it could pose a security threat to your cluster. That is why you have the network policy to protect you.

Network Policy

A network policy refers to a set of constraints, settings, and conditions that you have set that allow you to decide who is given permission to connect to your network. You can also specify the various circumstances that dictate when they can or cannot connect.

Your network policy acts as both an authorization procedure and an authentication process. This allows you to give only a certain set of users access to your cluster and containers. As you saw in the previous section, simply allowing an ingress point can be quite dangerous. This is why you need to set up a network security procedure in order to make sure that no kind of traffic enters your application. Once you have established the parameters, the network protocol performs all the necessary tasks on its own.

The best way to think of network policies is to consider them as rules. When a connection request is made, then the network protocol compares the rules that you have established to the request made. If all the conditions are met, then the user receives access. If not, then the user remains blocked from entering your application.

For Kubernetes, there are numerous network providers that are able to provide network policies. However, the one that we are going to use is Calico. Our first step is to download the application. You can do that here:

https:// github. com/ projectcalico/calico/ blob/ master/ v2. 4/ getting- started/kubernetes/ installation/ hosted/ calico.yaml)

Once you have done that, your next step is to discover the IP of etcd. You can use the below command to discover the IP address.

// find out etcd ip

 # minikube ssh -- "sudo /usr/local/bin/localkube --host-ip"

2017-07-27 04:10:58.941493 I | proto: duplicate proto type registered:

google.protobuf.Any

2017-07-27 04:10:58.941822 I | proto: duplicate proto type registered:

google.protobuf.Duration

2017-07-27 04:10:58.942028 I | proto: duplicate proto type registered:

google.protobuf.Timestamp

localkube host ip: 10.0.2.15

Source: (Baier, 2017)

Apart from the network security, you can also adjust the security settings on the containers.

Container Security

While Kubernetes plays an important role in providing convenience to improve the way developers work with containers, it does not do much for improving the security. This is not because of negligence on the part of Google. It is mainly because of the open-source nature of Kubernetes. One cannot place restrictions on the platform and then also give freedom to the developers to explore the platform.

Here are a few steps you can take to improve the security of the containers.

Method 1

Make sure that you are scanning the images for potential threats. Usually, the apps and images that you make use of on Kubernetes are without any threats. If you notice a threat, do not immediately delete the app. Do know that new flaws are always discovered. This is always the case with platforms that are constantly improving and developing. So make sure that you look at the community for help with certain images if you are not certain. Make sure that you are also updating the virus and vulnerability scan regularly in order to pick out threats faster.

Method 2

Be part of the Kubernetes community. Explore the forums and check out what new stuff they have to offer. You can explore more about their community right here: *https://kubernetes.io/community/*

Method 3

Sometimes, you might have deployed certain containers that have full access to the host operating system. In this case, have you protected yourself against any potential threats? These containers that have access to the host system are called privilege containers. If you have such containers, then you might have to be extra vigilant with them, ensuring that they are not breaching security in any way.

Method 4

Some container applications are exposed because they are outside the Kubernetes cluster. These applications offer a window for external threats to enter into the Kubernetes cluster. One of the best ways to prevent any potential attacks from outside is to close down any communication paths you have created for your Kubernetes container that might expose it to threats. At the same time, if you are aware of the potential threat that you might face, then you could also prepare a vulnerability scan that will detect those threats before they can cause any damage.

Method 5

Your work is not done until you have completed the production process. This means that certain malicious activities can cause harm to your containers during the production process. Make sure that you are prepared for it and have created restrictions on your containers.

Method 6

Finally, you need to know which team or developer has ownership of certain containerized applications. This is not because you would like to lay the blame on someone or hold people accountable. Rather, you are getting this information in order to reach out to the team or developer who will be able to help you discover the exact nature of the problem. Additionally, you will also be able to know where the vulnerability happened and help the team find fixes.

Method 7

Prioritize your vulnerabilities. This means that if you have been attacked by outside threats, then you cannot focus on them all. For example, let us say that you have 48 vulnerabilities to deal with. You can't go through each of them until you find the one that is causing the most harm. You could be dealing with vulnerability number 10 while number 31 is already creating even more damage. Look at all the vulnerabilities and try first to fix those that have the biggest threat.

Kubernetes Secrets

Secret is a special function in Kubernetes that allows you to store sensitive information. Such sensitive information includes passwords, tokens, SSH keys, and more. Rather than keep this information open to others, you can place them in secret, allowing a few people to have access to it.

So what is secret?

In Kubernetes, secret refers to an object that you can use to store small amounts of data, typically sensitive information like the ones that we mentioned above.

There are two ways to use secrets within a pod. The first method is to place the files in a volume and then mounting that volume on one of the containers within the pod. The other method is to use kubelet when you are pulling out the images for the pod.

Whenever the need arises for a component to make use of the information in the secret, it will utilize the file. Otherwise, the file will not be revealed to any user, except you.

How Can You Create a Secret?

You need to first create a secret in file using the yaml format. The secret usually contains two forms of maps. You can also use a text file, but if you do, then you have to use the following command:

$ kubectl create secret generic tomcat-passwd --from-file = ./username.txt --fromfile =./.password.txt

If you are using the yaml format, then you have to use this command:

$ kubectl create --f Secret.yaml

secrets/(secret file name)

Source: (Baier, 2017)

With just a few simple steps, you have created your secret. You can use the above steps every time you would like to create a secret and then store it on the system.

Best Practices When Handling Secret

Secrets are usually encrypted within the infrastructure of Kubernetes. However, if you pass them over to a workload, then they become transferred to plain text. This means that if anyone accessed the file at that point, they can easily see the sensitive information that you are trying to store. So make sure that you have permission to access the workload and no one else does.

Workloads can sometimes accidentally reveal the contents of the secret in the log files. Make sure that if a workload uses a secret, you check the log files to remove any traces of the information of the secret.

If you have changed the secret, then you need to restart the workload pods. In other words, if you have attached the secret to a container, then you need to restart it so that it can make use of the new secret.

Chapter 9: Administrative Clusters

One of the main purposes of using namespaces in Kubernetes is to ensure that you are driving resources taken from a physical cluster to various virtual ones. What this does is allow you to utilize different groups that share the same physical cluster.

Here are a few features of namespaces:

- The object name that you mention in each namespace is unique.
- You can set up quotes for the resources used by namespaces.
- Namespaces carry certain policies for authentication procedures.

Namespaces play an important role when different projects and teams within the same organization are working together. This way, each project or team has its own virtual cluster. These virtual clusters function in isolation, but they have the same physical cluster.

This is why it is important to create namespaces for your clusters. Here is a template that you can refer to in order to get started:

// configuration file of namespace

 # cat 8-1-1_ns1.yml

apiVersion: v1

kind: Namespace

metadata:

name: project1

// create namespace for project1

 # kubectl create -f 8-1-1_ns1.yml

namespace "project1" created

// list namespace, the abbreviation of namespaces is ns. We could use

`kubectl get ns` to list it as well.

 # kubectl get namespaces

NAME	STATUS	AGE
default	Active	1d
kube-public	Active	1d
kube-system	Active	1d
project1	Active	11s

Kubeconfig

Source: (Baier, 2017)

This is another important feature that you should be aware of. Kubeconfig gives you the ability to switch between multiple clusters easily. The way it does is by organizing the information about namespaces, users, clusters, and other important data.

When you have multiple clusters, then the users access each of them in different ways.

Think of a process similar to the process of filing. You have a cabinet and on the table in front of you are numerous files and folders. If you start tossing the files and folders into the cabinet, then you are going to arrange them rapidly. You have no idea if the files are arranged alphabetically or chronologically. Every time you would like to take one file, you have to go through all the files. This becomes a cumbersome task. But what if you had a method of identifying the files easily? You begin by providing each cabinet with a designation. For example, the top cabinet is A to J, the next one is of K to R, and so on. Within each cabinet, you arrange the files in such a way that a file with the name AA is arranged first, followed by AB, and so on. Now you have a system in place. You can easily get the exact file that you are looking for in a fraction of the time it would have taken were all the files jumbled and arranged haphazardly.

In order to make access easy, a kubeconfig uses what is known as a context. A context is nothing but the namespace that is used within a given cluster. Most of the operations within Kubernetes occur within a context. Because of this, when clients have the context, they know exactly which cluster and namespace they are working on. Just like the filing system, you do not have a way to easily reach the particular component.

Here is an example of a code that uses a Kubeconfig:

 # kubectl config view

```
apiVersion: v1

clusters:

- cluster:

certificate-authority: /Users/k8s/.minikube/ca.crt

server: https://192.168.99.100:8443

name: minikube

contexts:

- context:

cluster: minikube

user: minikube

name: minikube

current-context: minikube

kind: Config

preferences: {}

users:

- name: minikube

user:

client-certificate: /Users/k8s/.minikube/apiserver.crt

client-key: /Users/k8s/.minikube/apiserver.key
```

Source: (Baier, 2017)

In the above example, you have a cluster called minikube. Now that you have the name, any client who wishes to work on it can find it easily. Within the cluster, there would be many kubeconfig files for various components.

Authentication in Kubernetes

In Kubernetes, the idea of identity plays out a little differently than what you might be accustomed to when using other applications or platforms. Typically, you might think of an identity as a user portfolio or description. But in Kubernetes, identity refers to an API.

An API (or application programming interface) is like a door or a window to a particular software. This allows people to access the software without having the developer share details of the code of the software. Each time someone uses an API, it is different from the previous API. This means that it has its own access protocols.

So how does Kubernetes recognize you in such a manner?

It uses what is known as an OpenID connect to authenticate the user. This happens in a few steps.

The user first logs into the identity provider. For example, GCE.

You are then provided with an *id_token* and *refresh_token*.

You then use the *id_token* to let Kubernetes know that it is indeed you who is accessing the application.

After a while, the id_token expires. At this point, you can use the refresh_token to generate a new id_token. You can easily get a token if you are working on your GCE. As soon as you open your Google Cloud console, Google takes you to the consent screen. When the user approves, a new access token is generated.

Authorization in Kubernetes

You can use various authorization modules in Kubernetes. One of the most common ones is the ABAC, or Attribute Based Access Control.

ABAC allows the admin to create policies for user authorization. This means that when a user is trying to gain access to the application, he or she must meet a predetermined set of policies established by the administrator.

There are four main components of an ABAC:

- The subject
- Action
- Resource
- The request environment

Subject

The subject refers to the user who is requesting access to the asset. In this case, the asset refers to the application. There are various attributes that define the subject. For example, the company or department to which the user belongs, user ID, management level, roles, certifications, and many others. You can use these attributes to ensure that the user who is getting access to the application is really the one to whom you intend to provide the access. If you had decided that the IT

Manager named Mark is the one who is going to get access, then it is going to be only him who gains access. You cannot have another IT Manager named Alice or John try to gain access, since their attributes do not match the ones you had set up.

Action

This refers to what you allow the user to perform once he or she has access to your application. For example, you can give them the privilege to read and view the application. Alternatively, you can decide if you would like to give them the freedom to perform edits. It is all up to you.

Resource

This refers to the component or asset that is affected by the action carried out by the user. If you intend to give the user freedom to make changes to the component, then you can provide them with the required permission to do so.

Environment

Environment refers to various factors that determine how and where the client is trying to get access. Is the user using a laptop or a mobile device? Where is the user currently located? What is the time at the user's location? All of these factors determine the environment of the access. For example, you can provide the user access during the day and restrict access during the night, when you are not in front of the system to monitor the user's activity.

How do you determine the authorization?

You have to use a command when you first access the API. This means that if you have already accessed your application via the API, then you have to restart it in order to determine authorization. Once you have restarted the API, you simply have to use this command: *authorization-policy-file=<policy_file_name>*.

Chapter 10: Kubernetes and GCP

As you have gone through this book, you might have come across various concepts that require additional explanation. One of those concepts is Public Cloud.

So what exactly is it? How does it work?

Let us take a look.

What Is Public Cloud?

When you are unable to perform certain computing functions or services on your computer or laptop, then you make use of a public cloud facility. Public cloud is an umbrella term that refers to any service that is offered by a third party over an internet. This means that the service is publicly available for anyone to use or purchase.

Let us take a simple example. Imagine that you would like to edit videos but your laptop does not have the computing power to work with any of the popular video editing software. Since you cannot directly use the software on your computer, you can search online for a similar application that you do not have to download onto your computer and that you can use within a web browser.

There are many services that make use of the public cloud system. In fact, even Google Docs is a form of public cloud service. You are using a Word processor on the server of a third party. In this case, that third party just so happens to be Google.

One of the main benefits of public cloud services is that they save a lot of money for people and organizations who cannot afford to purchase original software. Usually public cloud services offer various benefits.

If you were to purchase a software, then you can install that software on one device only. However, in a public cloud, you can pay the same price that you paid for the service (or even less), and then allow more than one person to make use of the service. Additionally, any individual can make use of the service from any location.

A public cloud can also be deployed much faster. Once all the users are connected, then it is only a matter of providing their credentials and then logging into the profile. Once everyone is connected, the work can begin.

What Is GCP?

GCP is the abbreviated form of Google Cloud Platform. It is similar to the public cloud application that we were talking about in the previous section. Essentially, it is a platform that provides a collection of Google services. The platform provides you with numerous services including networking, storage, computing, and more. You will have all the necessary features and facilities to help you with your Kubernetes program.

Let's get solving

Build scalable apps. Use Google's global, reliable infrastructure. Securely manage enterprise data. Get insights from data faster. Whatever you're solving for, Google Cloud can help.

Get started for free   Contact sales

You can get started on Google Cloud Platform for free for a test run.

So why exactly do we need Google cloud? Why can't we use any other cloud?

There are three main reasons for using Google cloud.

- It offers you GCE, which is essentially what you will be using for Kubernetes.
- It also provides you with Google Cloud Storage. This will be useful for storing various components of your application.
- FInally, it offers a customer-friendly form of pricing structure. This is why many organizations and users opt for GCE, since it offers a great bang for your buck.

Since you are going to be using Kubernetes on the GCE, you can easily access your GCP by going to this link: *https://console.cloud.google.com/getting-started.*

Components of GCP

GCP comes packed with various components that you can make use of. Let us examine some of them.

Compute Services

Google App Engine

You can use this platform to launch applications, PHP, or Java. This cloud computing service allows you to create and host web applications for those centers that are managed by Google.

Compute Engine

Here, you can run Linux virtual machines.

Kubernetes Engine

This component provides the platform for operations, scaling, and deployment of applications across numerous hosts. It also comes packed with numerous container tools, including the one we have been discussing in this book, Docker.

Storage Services

Google Cloud Storage

This is an online storage platform storing data on the Google infrastructure. If you have a large amount of data that you would like to store somewhere other than your device, then you can make use of Google Cloud.

Cloud SQL

You can use this service in order to create and configure various databases that are in Google Cloud.

Cloud Bigtable

This is an incredibly fast and highly scalable infrastructure for database management.

Networking

BigQuery

Google BigQuery is a service that provides analysis to help businesses and organizations understand data.

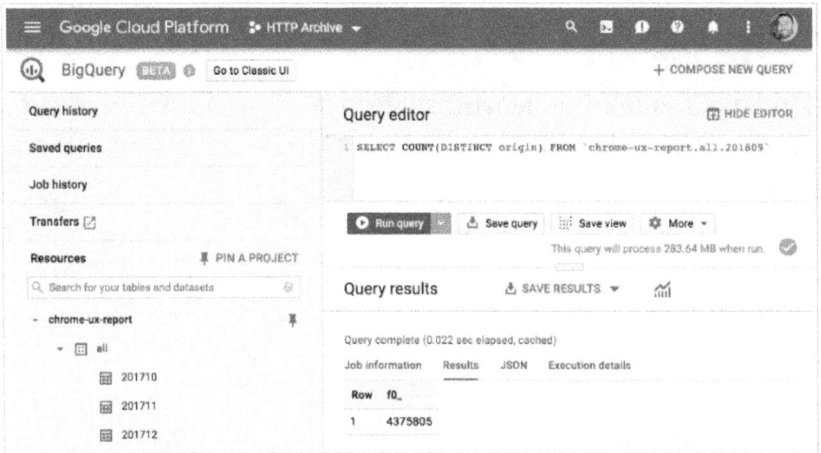

BigQuery gives you many options to create a customized report.

Google Cloud Data Storage

This is a datastore that you can fully manage and which provides various features.

Google Cloud Dataproc

This service allows for data processing. You can also utilize other services like Hadopp to create clusters and then manage them. And can create workloads exactly when you require them.

Cloud AI

Cloud Machine Learning Engine

You can use this service in order to design and build machine learning models.

Cloud AutoML

This is a machine learning service that allows users to provide their data sets and allow Google to evaluate those sets.

Management Tools

Google Stackdriver

This service provides you with diagnostics and performance data through logging, monitoring, error reporting, and tracing.

Google Cloud Console App

A mobile application that allows users to gain access to many of Google's Cloud services through a mobile device.

Identity and Security

Cloud Data Loss Prevention API

You can use this service in order to manage your sensitive data. It provides easy and safe classification of various data, including credit card numbers, passport numbers, and other sensitive information.

Cloud IAM

Cloud Identity and Access Management established a set of policies that ensure that the right people with the right credentials are given access to the resources on the Google Cloud platform.

Chapter 11: Kubernetes and AWS

Some users might use AWS instead of the Google Cloud platform. If you are opting to work on AWS, then here is how you can get started on the platform.

First things first. What exactly is AWS?

You can think of AWS as a cloud platform similar to Google, except that this platform is provided by Amazon. It has many of the features that you can find on Google, including services such as networking, storage, database, messaging, and even compute.

The Amazon Web Services also makes use of the EC2 console, which is a special console that you utilize to work with Kubernetes.

Getting Started With Kops

Here is how you can get started on AWS. You need to first set up kops, which is nothing but a shortened version of Kubernetes Operations. It is an open source project that allows you to setup Kubernetes clusters easily on a particular platform. In this case, we can use the AWS as the platform and run kops on it.

You can easily download kops from here: *https://github.com/kubernetes/kops.*

Next, you simply have to run kops and allow it to complete the installation process.

And that is all there is to it! Once you have installed kops, you are ready to start working on Kubernetes using the AWS platform.

Once you have gotten set up, you need to then ensure that you have used AWS as the cloud provider of kops. What this means is that when you are using the LoadBalancer feature, the application will have use of the Elastic Load Balancing (ELB), which is Amazon's version of the LoadBalancer. Since you are working within the AWS infrastructure, it is important that you work with the LoadBalancer of that infrastructure.

To define the load balancer, you simply have to navigate to the Amazon EC2.

Head over to the navigation bar and then select the region for the load balancer. If you had selected a region when you set up the VM on the EC2, then make sure that you select the same region or else the load balancer won't function properly.

You should see the option LOAD BALANCING in the navigation pane. Click on it and choose Load Balancers.

Next click on Create Load Balancer and then choose Classic Load Balancer. Click on Create. You are good to go!

Initial Setup

When you first set up AWS, your account will be used for all of the services on Amazon. In order to create your account, you need to first navigate to *https://portal.aws.amazon.com/billing/signup*. Once you reach the platform, you are going to discover instructions that help you create the account. Use them to finalize the billing method and other details required for creating your account.

Your account creation process might involve a phone call where you have to enter the code that is provided in the call on the keypad of your mobile device.

You will then be provided with an AWS account ID. This is important, so make sure you note down the ID.

Next, you will need to create an IAM user account. As soon as you login into your AWS account, you should be able to see your IAM console. If you cannot, then you can use this link: *https://console.aws.amazon.com/iam*

Once you have created an account on IAM, you are ready to start using AWS services.

Benefits of AWS

How can AWS help you with Kubernetes? There are a few benefits that can greatly compel someone to make use of the AWS services.

One of the main advantages of AWS is that it is easy to use. New users might find that many of the features are easy to understand and the menus are designed to be accessible.

When organizations launch projects, they are often unsure how much space they will require. AWS can help them with this problem by offering low costs for a large space. This way, organizations don't have to worry that they won't have enough space or that they might have to pay more for a large space.

AWS also provides great speed to the user. Enterprises are often in the dark when it comes to knowing how long it takes to get a server. In most cases, it could take up to 1 week for them to hire a server. In cases of AWS, users receive a server within a matter of minutes.

AWS also provides a high level of security to the data stored within its database. The added benefit is that users can take advantage of this benefit without a high additional cost.

Conclusion

Ask any modern software developer, and he or she will attest to the fact that containers have provided them with more flexibility in order to run applications on virtual and physical environments.

Because of containers, you are able to easily make your applications portable. You can develop them for different environments and get them ready for the testing phase instantly. The whole process, from development to final version, is made much smoother with the use of containers.

You can even increase application processes in order to meet demand. You don't have to wait on long processes that consume time and yield far poorer resources than containers. After all, when you are using containers, you have so much accessibility that you are able to immediately modify, change, or update your application before users even begin to access it.

But what makes Kubernetes so important to developers today?

Open-Source

Because Kubernetes is an open-source platform, you can take advantage of various tools in order to aid the development of your application. When an application is open-source, then various resources can pool together in order to solve a problem or discover a new application feature. In fact, you can get the community to help you with various projects and applications. They can take a look at something, tinker with it, and find solutions that you might not have thought of earlier. One of the most popular platforms that is open-source is the Android App Store. Anyone can develop an application and publish it on the app store. This is why you are more likely to find free software in an Android app store than in the iOS version.

Portable

Kubernetes allows you to deploy your applications faster because you can make use of multiple cloud providers for your application. You can work on your application from another laptop without any issues. Simply log into your GCE and continue your progress from where you left off.

Better Management

When you are using containers, then you are making use of small components. This allows you to manage them easily. Because of the feature of pods–where a collection of containers are under the control of a single application–that add convenience to containers, you can easily isolate containers into different groups. This allows you to work on different aspects of your application with ease.

But most importantly, developers love Kubernetes. They have discovered that the entire platform can take their application from one environment to another with ease.

It is no wonder that Kubernetes has now become the industry standard when it comes to deploying containers. It is true that the technology has been in existence for some time now.

However, when it was initially launched, it was faced with much skepticism. Over time, as more and more developers began to use it and fine tune it (since it is open-source), it has become an invaluable part of various vendors and projects. Even organizations have now become comfortable adopting Kubernetes because it helps them avoid cramming too many processes into a single project.

Then there is the fact that Kubernetes was developed by Google. The tech giant knows how to fix bugs and other problems with their software. You know that if you find any issues with Kubernetes, it won't be long before the problem has a solution. Furthermore, when you combine the efforts of not just Google, but other developers from the community who have years of experience, then you have a myriad of tools, assistance, and functions that you can use to your advantage.

Given the interest in containers, there are other platforms that are built around orchestration and management tools. These platforms are trying to emulate the success that older Kubernetes platforms such as GCE have enjoyed. We have already looked at some of the other alternatives, such as HashiCorp and AWS.

All of the above points come to one conclusion: the future of application development lies with Kubernetes. There is a reason that developers are spending their time and resources to understand the platform better. It is not only because it works well with various business goals, but it provides the sort of conveniences that developers look for in other platforms.

CPSIA information can be obtained
at www.ICGtesting.com
Printed in the USA
LVHW050725271220
675069LV00013B/358